Lizzie Nunnery's … rpool Everyman, 2007) … Meyer-Whitworth Award. She co-wro… , winner of the Amnesty International Award … dom of Expression (Everyman/ Traverse, Edinburgh, 2006). *The Swallowing Dark* (Liverpool Playhouse Studio/Theatre503, 2011) was shortlisted for the Susan Smith Blackburn Award, as was her play with songs *Narvik* (Box of Tricks, national tour Jan–March 2017). After *The Sum*, forthcoming work includes *Horny Handed Tons of Soil* (Unity Theatre, Liverpool, July 2017, national tour Sept–Nov 2017). She has written extensively for BBC radio and is also a poet, singer and songwriter, performing regularly with producer/composer Vidar Norheim.

also by Lizzie Nunnery from Faber

INTEMPERANCE
NARVIK

LIZZIE NUNNERY

The Sum

a play with songs

FABER & FABER

First published in 2017

by Faber and Faber Limited
74–77 Great Russell Street, London WC1B 3DA

Typeset by Country Setting, Kingsdown, Kent CT14 8ES
Printed in England by CPI Group (UK) Ltd, Croydon CR0 4YY

A CIP record for this book is available from the British Library

ISBN 978-0-571-34004-0

MIX
Paper from responsible sources
FSC® C013604
www.fsc.org

2 4 6 8 10 9 7 5 3 1

For Rita, my Mum

Acknowledgements

Thank you to Suzanne Bell, Cora Bissett, Craig Gilbert, Hayley Greggs, Laura Hall, Bryony Lavery, Sarah Nunnery Jones, Jane Owens at the Citizens Advice Bureau, Helen Perry, Lindsay Rodden, Sue Troake, the women of the Epsy Centre, and all actors who contributed to the development of the piece.

The play was originally developed through the Bruntwood Salon Playwrights scheme as part of the Bruntwood Hub at the Royal Exchange Theatre and Liverpool Everyman and Playhouse.

The Sum was first performed at the Everyman Theatre, Liverpool, on 6 May 2017. The cast was as follows:

Alan McClasker Patrick Brennan
Paul Walsh George Caple
Iris Brennan Pauline Daniels
Eve Brennan Laura Dos Santos
Lisa Brennan Emily Hughes
Ismael Tengku Tom Kanji
Faisa Ahmed Asha Kingsley
Theresa Tago Melanie La Barrie
Bryn Hughes Dean Nolan
Gabi Kalnietis Zelina Rebeiro
Steph O'Sullivan Keddy Sutton
Danny Scott Liam Tobin

Director Gemma Bodinetz
Composer and Musical Director Vidar Norheim
Designers Molly Elizabeth Lacey Davies, Jocelyn Meall and Michael Vale
Lighting Designer Aideen Malone
Sound Designer Fergus O'Hare
Choreographer Charlotte Broom
Musician Martin Heslop
Costume Supervisor Jacquie Davies
Associate Director Chris Tomlinson
Associate Lighting Designer Kay Haynes
YEP Assistant Director Chantell Walker
Casting Director Sam Stevenson

Characters

Eve Brennan
thirty-one, from Liverpool 8

Danny Scott
thirty-one, from Liverpool 8

Lisa Brennan
fourteen, Eve's daughter

Alan McClasker
forty, from Lancashire

Iris Brennan
sixty-four, Eve's mum

The Staff

Steph O'Sullivan
thirties, from Liverpool 8

Theresa Tago
fifties, non-white, from Trinidad

Gabi Kalnietis
twenties, Lithuanian descent, from Liverpool 8

Faisa Ahmed
twenties, Muslim, from Iran

Ismael Tengku
forties, Malaysian

Bryn Hughes
thirties,Welsh

Paul Walsh
twenties, from Liverpool

Songs

1 Forgive Me If I Smile: Scene 1
2 Whole Again: Scene 3 (reprise Scenes 9, 23)
3 Dawn Light: Scene 5
4 Magical Times: Scene 6 (reprise Scenes 19, 22)
5 Zero Hour Blues: Scene 8
6 Sand: Scene 8
7 Why Have It Hard? Scene 11 (reprise Scene 16)
8 One Day I Want to Get Straight: Scene 12
9 Smile and a Knife: Scene 13
10 Where's Your Soul? Scene 17 (reprise Scene 21)
11 Poverty Knocks: Scene 23

Lyrics by Lizzie Nunnery

Music by Lizzie Nunnery/Vidar Norheim

For musical scores apply to the writer's agent

THE SUM

The Set

The assorted contents of a life:
heaps of clothes, crockery, ornaments,
books, loose photographs, cutlery, plant pots, tins,
dried food, wine bottles, glasses, ill-matching
furniture including a bed, table and armchair –
nothing of much financial worth. Amongst
all this are various musical instruments.
All locations are created from this jumble.

Notes

A dash (–) at the end of a line indicates
an interruption

An ellipsis (. . .) indicates a search
for a thought or words

SCENE ONE
FORGIVE ME IF I SMILE

Eve surrounded by darkness, working out maths with a pen and paper.

Eve . . . Plus 65p for a loaf of bread + £1.52 mild cheddar + £1.45 rice + £1.80 for a tin of tuna + £2 bag of apples + £1.36 frozen mince = £220.63. (*Beat.*) I'm a number's person. Always have been. Give me a sum, I can do it. Give me a spreadsheet, I can balance it. And everything's a balance: time and money and energy, work and home and sleeping and waking. Wanting and planning.

Lights broaden on a hardware superstore, late afternoon. Eve is at a desk in the office. Paul and Bryn stack tins of paint. Ismael pushes trolleys of goods, unloads them. Theresa mops floors. Steph puts a cup of tea on Eve's desk. As Steph moves away Eve squeezes her hand. Gabi and Faisa check prices/stock levels with scanners. Steph joins Theresa mopping up/ wiping surfaces.

Paul (*calling to Gabi*) Go on then, what do you reckon?

Bryn It's a contradiction in terms, Paul.

Paul I'm not asking you, I'm asking Gabi.

Gabi (*distracted*) You're what?

Paul What's your best ever day at work?

Gabi This one, here with you now.

Paul Really?

Gabi (*sarcastic*) Yeah, this morning I walked across the car park in the rain at 5.30 a.m. and thought, 'Today is the best day of my life.'

Paul Did you?

Bryn (*low*) Come on, lad, just leave it.

Paul My mum says if I'm gonna get to know people here I have to ask questions.

Bryn Yeah, but you don't ask the same question over and over again.

Paul Gabi . . .

Bryn (*low to Paul*) Best way to get a woman to want you, boy: ignore her completely.

Paul looks at Bryn in confusion.

Faisa Extra zero day. None of your days beat that.

Bryn You what?

Faisa In here last New Year's Day – I check my balance for my overtime. It's there. But it's not twenty pounds, it's two hundred pounds.

Steph No way.

Faisa I run out those doors, jump a taxi to Cash Converters on Smithdown – I know exactly what I'm buying.

He holds up his wrist, light bounces off his watch.

All my life I wanted a nice gold watch: something people would look at and say . . . *nice*.

Bryn Did Alan get on to it?

Faisa Of course he did, but it was his mistake, and by then I'd spent the money.

The others laugh or cheer.

Gabi You know you can get the time on your phone these days, Ismael?

Theresa When Thatcher went! Eh, Steph? When it came on the radio: all of us just standing here, mouths hanging open –

Steph With the shock and the fucking joy of it.

Faisa I don't want to hear this.

Steph You can't understand, love.

Faisa It's a woman dead.

Bryn Agreed. Dance on the grave of the dead and expect no mercy from any soul. (*Beat.*) Cracking night down the pub though.

Theresa and Steph laugh. Bryn grins at them.

Paul My mum talks about Thatcher – her lips go all tight and blue.

Alan enters quickly, frowning, looking around.

Faisa What she did she did. It's done. Wallowers: all of you.

Steph It's not done and it's not dead.

Alan Have you seen Eve?

Steph Office. Doing the payroll.

Paul What's your best ever day at work, Alan?

Alan Er . . . Fridays.

They all laugh. Alan looks at them bewildered as he moves off to find Eve.

Shift finished one minute ago. You can gas all you like, but you're on your own time.

Gabi pulls a face at Alan. Steph, Faisa and Theresa laugh at this as they all move off. Bryn jumps on the back of a trolley and scoots off. Paul and Ismael follow.

Alan (*calling after them*) Actually, not you, Theresa. Customer loo's in a right state.

Theresa No one ever uses it.

Alan Because it's in a right state.

Theresa scowls at him, moves upstage with her mop and bucket, continues cleaning. Alan approaches the office.

Eve £192.63 for gas, water, electric, TV licence, council tax + £520 rent = £712.63. Lisa's pocket money, bus fare, school dinners, science club, books, PE kit, direct debits on the laptop = £445.22. Plus £51.30 for my travel, £40 for toiletries, £10 for the holiday fund, £19 broadband, £74.68 in phone bills + four quid for the window cleaner= £644.20. Credit cards plus store cards plus insurance = £389.06. £712.63 + £644.20 –

Alan (*popping his head in*) Eve?

Eve Plus £389.06 + £220.63 =

Alan Can I have a minute? Five minutes that's all. Fifteen max.

Eve Just give me a sec . . .

Alan Only it's, er . . . It's . . .

Eve You alright, Al?

Alan No, it's . . . I mean yes. I'm okay. We're alright.

Eve We? Like the royal 'we'?

Alan That's a nice dress.

Eve It's a blouse and skirt.

Alan You got it for your birthday. I remember.

Eve Al?

Alan I remember you saying . . .

Eve Has something happened?

Alan No. Well . . . in a sense. I, er . . . Eve . . .

She looks at him, waiting.

I'm doing my best here. You know that?

Eve (*going to him*) Course you are.

Alan I'm doing my best, Eve.

Eve (*ushering him in*) We all have heavy days. You're not invincible.

Alan Exactly. Exactly, I'm not.

Eve My dad died thirteen years ago, it still gets on top of me sometimes. What's it been – a year?

Alan It's not that. It's not –

Eve It's one foot in front of the other. Right? Eyes front, chin up – ignore all the shit they talk out there in the shop.

Alan What shit?

Eve Plaster on a smile and eventually it *will* start to feel better.

Alan They're talking about *me*?

Eve You're doing everything he would've wanted. You're still here running this place –

Alan Oh, *Christ*.

Eve What? Al, *what*?

He takes her cup of tea, drinks from it.

Alan I've had phone calls. From the board. Emails bouncing around . . .

Eve What's the genius idea this time? Rebrand the trolleys? Digitalise the garden section?

Alan They're nervous. Investors are nervous. Which makes the shareholders nervous.

Eve Should *I* be nervous?

Alan They want us more flexible. Competitive. Light on our feet.

Eve We're selling paint, not doing gymnastics.

Alan We need to generate confidence –

Eve We've had a few bad months, that's all –

Alan Profit margins are out of balance with staffing levels –

Eve You're doing that thing, Al: you're speaking words but you're not actually saying anything.

He stares at her.

Are you firing me?

Alan *No*. God, no.

Eve Look me in the eye.

Alan I'm modernising. Restructuring.

Eve You're cutting hours?

He looks at her, nods.

Everyone's hours?

Alan This isn't me. This is share prices dropping and investors bailing, directors looking round the portfolio for fat to cut away. They're shitting themselves over the referendum –

Eve *Everyone's* hours?

Alan Just for now. Just until I can show a clean sheet.

Eve My hours?

Alan Just by a couple of days a week.

Eve A *couple of days*?

Alan Just until things pick up. Just for a month or so.

Eve No. No, let's think about this.

Alan I'll be telling the same to the Aintree and Garston staff –

Eve You know my mum hasn't been well. She's not working and –

Alan We need to get more –

Eve Don't say the word 'flexible' again.

Alan I just need time. I just need you to help me.

Eve We'll tell them to hold off. We'll bring in some new lines. August bank holiday's coming up –

Alan It's not enough. You think I haven't tried –?

Eve If the place wasn't falling to bits more people might come in here.

Alan That's not going to wash. That's not going to work for them.

Eve It's your name above the door.

Alan And I take full responsibility. Not one person's losing their job.

Eve *Everyone's* hours?

Alan It's the contract you all signed. Nothing was ever set in stone.

The phone rings. She moves to leave. Alan slams the phone against the receiver to stop it.

This isn't me, Eve. You know that?

Eve One month?

Alan Eh?

Eve You said a month?

Alan This is my place. This is *our* place. I . . .

She nods.

First step's getting the message out there.

Eve No. Not me –

Alan They like you. They trust you.

Eve And I can't tell them it's a good thing that they're losing hours.

Alan You tell them it's the best we've got. They'll believe it from you.

Eve This is shit, Alan.

The phone rings again.

Alan It is. But sometimes we have to swallow shit. With a little bit of sugar. (*Picking up phone.*) Alan McClasker? (*Beat.*) Yeah she's . . . Okay. Okay.

He hands the phone to Eve.

Eve Hello? (*Her face falls.*) He's what?

Lights down on Eve and Alan, up on Theresa as she mops. The band plays. Gabi, Steph and Faisa enter and begin to help Theresa.

Theresa (*sung*)
Not wishing to be cruel, not wishing to be crass
But I heard the news break like the tinkling of glass
She closed the docks and kept the change
And took her tea with Pinochet
So forgive me if I smile . . .

Gabi/Steph
Forgive me if I smile . . .

Theresa/Gabi/Steph
Forgive me if I smiled the day that Maggie Thatcher died

The rest of the staff enter.

Theresa (*sung*)
Not wanting to be maudlin

Gabi/Steph
Not wishing to offend

Theresa
But she crippled us with crafty tax
She sold us runner, sleeper, track
And that old train's not coming back
So forgive me if I smile . . .

Gabi/Steph
Forgive me if I smile . . .

Theresa/Gabi/Steph
Forgive me if I smiled the day that Maggie Thatcher died

Chorus.

Faisa
Old noise, old news

Steph
Here we all are again

Gabi
You can't wipe that slate clean

Theresa
New blood from old wounds

Steph
Here we all are again

Gabi
You can't wipe that slate clean

Theresa (*sung*)
She took our wage and sent it south
She took milk from our children's mouths
And made our streets a battleground
So forgive me if I smile . . .

Gabi/Steph
Forgive me if I smile . . .

Theresa/Gabi/Steph
Forgive me if I smiled the day that Maggie Thatcher died

Faisa
There's a hollow refrain
To your victory tune

Theresa/Gabi/Steph
There's a voice in your ear and it
May be familiar to

Theresa
You . . .

Faisa/Bryn/Paul/Ismael
Old noise, old news

Steph
Here we all are again

Gabi/Bryn/Paul/Ismael
You can't
Wipe that slate clean

Theresa/Bryn/Paul/Ismael
New blood from old wounds

Steph
Here we all are again

Gabi/Bryn/Paul/Ismael
You can't
Wipe that slate clean

Repeat chorus.

Faisa/Bryn/Paul/Ismael
New blood, old wounds

Steph
Here we all are again

Theresa/Faisa
Forgive me if I smile

Repeat.

All
Here we all are again

Lights cut.

SCENE TWO
THE CRASH

Eve and Danny's kitchen. Danny sits. His right hand is bandaged. His face is badly bruised and grazed. Eve stands with her coat on.

Eve Let me see your hand.

Danny It's just a cut. I'm fine.

Eve What are you doing discharging yourself? The state of you.

Danny Sweetheart, I'm alright.

Eve Have you seen your face, Danny?

Danny I don't mind it . . . Makes me look tough.

Eve What even happened?

Danny I lost concentration. Hit a bump. You think I look bad, you should've seen the van.

She pulls him to her suddenly, holding on to him.

Eh . . . Evie . . . Look at me . . . I'm sat here, aren't I?

Eve You should be dead.

Danny Thanks very much.

Eve I get a message saying you're unconscious, you're in an ambulance –

Danny I'm sorry.

He hugs her.

Eve You 'lost concentration'?

Danny It came on the radio. About the girl.

Eve The girl?

Danny The MP. That poor woman – stabbed and shot in the street and . . . I don't know – I could *see* it.

Eve Danny . . .

Danny I'm driving and thinking, is this the start of something? Like is something coming unstuck? And there was this weight on my chest. And then this bastard speed bump came out of nowhere –

Eve Danny, you silly sod.

Danny Your dad used to speak round there. When the strike was on. Little towns like that – crowds all clapping.

Eve A lad got shot three streets away last summer. You didn't have a panic attack then.

Danny This is bigger, Evie. You've got to see this is bigger?

Eve (*taking his face in her hands*) The sky is not falling in. The Queen is not a shape-shifting lizard. The aliens are not in the White House.

She kisses him. He smiles at her.

Danny They might be though.

Eve It's one more nutter. There's always a nutter.

Iris enters the yard, takes a trowel and digs up flowers, clattering and cursing at intervals.

What did Tommo say about the van?

Danny Nothing.

Eve He's not making you pay for it?

Danny No. (*Beat.*) No.

Eve I'll talk to Lisa before she sees you. (*Turning to go.*) Don't want you scaring her with your clown eye.

Danny He sacked me, Evie.

Eve What?

Danny Tommo. He rang me in the hospital.

Eve He can't do that.

Danny He's been looking for reasons to get rid of people for –

Eve He can't sack you for –

Danny Said I had to be speeding. Reckons he could prove it.

Eve Were you speeding?

Danny He's on the radio every ten seconds telling me I'm late.

Eve That's not what I asked.

Danny This way he doesn't have to pay redundancy.

Eve No, of course – It's not your fault, it's a conspiracy, it's the state of the nation.

Noises from out in the yard get louder.

Danny (*peering out at Iris*) What's she doing now?

Eve Right, what's the plan? How are we gonna do without your wage?

Danny She's digging all my dahlias out the pots.

Eve I don't care what she's doing.

Danny The work I've put in to that yard –

Eve (*heading for the door*) She can wear them as a hat for all I care.

Danny *Evie, I'm sorry.* I am.

Pause. She stops. During the following Iris becomes distracted and wanders away.

Eve Alan's cut all the hours. I'm on three days a week as of Monday.

Danny So it's been a shit day.

Eve Where's next month's rent coming from?

Danny I'll have something sorted by then. Everyone needs a driver.

Eve Nice reference Tommo'll give you.

Danny I can do other things.

Eve Maybe something in a warehouse? I could ask Faisa's fella.

Danny I did woodwork at school. I made an ashtray.

Eve You'll be an ashtray-maker?

Danny An artisan, thank you very much. I'll sell quality ash receptacles to the Toxteth community.

Eve I remember that ashtray. It went on fire.

Danny I could start DJ-ing again. Used to make a good few bob.

Eve You used to come home with a fiver and a grin after buying your mates drinks all night.

Danny But you fancied me, didn't you? Behind them decks?

Eve I was the only one.

He laughs, goes to her.

You're a soft touch, Danny: that's your problem.

Danny What was it your dad used to say?

Eve Remind me.

Danny Are we breathing? Are we upright?

Eve Just about in your case.

Danny Then we're fighting.

Beat. She smiles at him.

Eve Then we're fighting.

SCENE THREE
PROTEST

Danny and Lisa move forward with placards, humming 'Whole Again'. Danny's placard reads: VOTE REMAIN, *Lisa's* CUT WAR NOT WELFARE. *The staff perform tasks as in Scene One. The band plays a fast percussive beat. Stark light as Eve sits with bills, pen, paper before her.*

Eve Three days a week = 25 hours at £7.20 per hour = £708 per month after tax. Tax credits + child benefit, housing benefit, council tax reduction = £838.08 a month. Add 189.30 Danny's back pay and I've got £1,735.38 going in, £1,966.52 going out . . . Deficit: £231.14. (*Beat.*) Okay, okay . . . Cuts . . . I need cuts. £10 for Lisa's pocket money (she'll understand); £10 holiday fund (forget that); £20 off the phone bills (no data), £30.25 for the credit card (we'll run up debt for now). Still £161 under . . .

She leafs through her notes, bills, searching for cuts.

Can't have the lights go off. Can't have the heat go out. Can't have Lisa getting behind at school. Can't have the bailiffs banging . . . We could go without biscuits, meat, chocolate . . . £15 pounds off the food bill. I could make stews, freeze them – a little bit every day. £25 pounds off. We could do porridge for breakfast – UHT milk. I could miss lunch. £43 off the food bill – why not? We can manage. Get it down to £44 a week. That leaves £1,853.27 going out, £1,735.38 going in. Deficit: £117.89. (*Beat.*) £117.89 under.

Danny/Lisa/The Staff

One of these days I'm gonna rant and rail
One of these days I'll be whole again (*Repeat.*)
These days, these days I'm gonna rant and rail
One of these days I'll be whole again (*Repeat.*)

Lights down on Eve. Lights down on the staff as the song ends. Danny and Lisa sit down on a kerb holding their signs. A crowd can be heard gathering up the road, slogans shouted.

Danny It'll be good, this – once the north Liverpool lot join up. We'll get the speeches going.

Lisa You don't have to sell it to me, Danny. I'm here, aren't I?

Danny We could keep out the house all day if you like. Go down the park?

Lisa And do what?

Danny Kick a ball about. Sit off and eat ice lollies. Scare the ducks.

Lisa I'm not twelve.

Danny Neither am I.

Lisa Sometimes I wonder.

Danny digs in his pocket, brings out half a cereal bar, takes a bite, offers it to Lisa.

It's got a hair on it.

Danny Extra protein.

She takes it, takes a bite, looking round.

Lisa Could we not've co-ordinated a bit more? We've got 'Vote Remain', 'Save Sefton Park Meadows', 'Stop the Badger Cull' –

Danny Everything's connected.

Lisa Some things are more connected than others. Why don't we just write on a placard 'Anything Bad' and have done?

Danny I'll leave you at home with your nan next time.

Lisa Don't joke about Nan.

Danny I know it's crap – her taking your room and all that.

Lisa You heard her call me Jimmy this morning?

Danny That was your grandad's name.

Lisa It's not my name, is it?

Danny She's alright.

Lisa She's not, you know? She had me turning the house upside down yesterday looking for a pair of shoes.

Danny What's wrong with that?

Lisa She was already wearing them.

Danny smiles in spite of himself.

What's funny about that?

Danny Nothing. *Nothing.* (*Beat.*) I thought it'd be a nice thing. Us doing this – like we used to –

Lisa It is nice. I'm having a really nice time. Stop going on about it.

Danny If this is about school . . . About this row. Your mum's been in and –

Lisa It wasn't a row.

Danny Look, this is me as your mate, trying to help you out.

Lisa Alright, *mate*: go ahead.

Danny Whatever happened to your bag?

Lisa Michelle Carter threw it on the roof.

Danny Well whatever it was – a little falling out between friends –

Lisa She's not my friend.

Danny This is what I'm saying – if you show you're alright with her –

Lisa She'll be alright with me?

Danny Exactly.

Lisa You know how when you're dead little you think you're the same as everyone else? Your family: the stuff you do and the stuff you have. You think everyone must be basically the same.

Danny And they are, aren't they?

Lisa No. They're not. We're not.

Danny What do you mean?

Lisa I'm a weirdo, Danny.

Danny Who says?

Lisa I'm a screff and a weirdo. Fact.

Danny This is this Michelle?

Lisa She's not even the worst. Amy Caldwell tried to push me down the stairs on Wednesday.

Danny She *what*?

Lisa Kelly McAllister shoved my books in the sink in biology lab – turned the taps on.

Danny Well, can't you get your mates involved – get them to say something?

Lisa Who says I've got mates?

Danny What about that short girl? Always hanging round eating crisps? *Ruby.*

Lisa *Ruth.* She went to bottom sets, I went to top sets. She doesn't speak to me now.

Danny She never did seem very bright.

Lisa Don't worry, I'm not asking you to *do* anything, Danny.

The north Liverpool protestors can be heard arriving up the road – horns blasting, muffled voices through loudhailers: 'Axe, axe, axe the bedroom tax.' Lisa and Danny look towards it.

Danny Here's what you do: you find the people like you. The other girls who aren't having a good time. You . . . organise. Band together over collective grievances. 'Cause if you're looking out for their interests, they're looking out for yours and then when these dickhea— (*Stopping himself.*) When these other girls try and have a pop at you, you've got support, haven't you? Solidarity. What you smiling at?

Lisa Nothing. It's nice.

Danny What's nice?

Lisa You are. It's nice you think like that.

Danny Are you patronising me?

Lisa It's not how it is.

Danny You're not telling me you're the only one they're picking on?

Lisa It's like . . . there are big kids and little kids . . . and fat kids and weird kids and kids with good clothes and kids dressed like tramps and kids who stink and kids who everyone fancies, and clever kids and stupid kids and everyone's just . . . getting their head down, getting through it. There's people who can stand up in the canteen and make a joke and everyone laughs and people who can't walk between classrooms without getting spat at. And everyone's trying so hard not to be the one that gets spat at . . . Everyone's looking around all the time . . . for stuff they can use, you know? And if I'm the one that everyone else has got the most shit on – then that's just who I am. It's just how it is.

Danny What have they got on you?

Lisa Everything. I use too many big words, I hand my homework in on time, I've been seen reading books, I answer questions in physics lessons –

Danny Well, you could knock that on the head.

Lisa Not when Mr Wan's cornering me. You want me to get them wrong on purpose?

Danny Maybe just for a couple of lessons?

Lisa I don't think that's what you're supposed to tell me, Danny.

Danny Well if you won't help yourself . . .

Lisa And then Nan . . .

Danny What about her?

Lisa Last term: I'm sitting on the field at break time and there she is coming towards me in her slippers, holding out a lunch box shouting, 'Where's little Lisa?'

Danny Oh Jesus . . .

Lisa And just crowds, just waves of kids following her laughing, screaming, 'Lisa! Lisa! You forgot your sarnies!' I can take them saying things about me but when it's her . . .

Danny Oh Jesus Christ . . .

Lisa Who am I gonna ask to stand up for me? Who's gonna be that stupid? I wouldn't be.

Danny Don't say that.

Lisa It's true.

Danny You're too clever, that's your problem. If it was me you know I'd probably just belt someone. And then belt someone else.

Lisa Well I'm not you, am I? I'm nothing like you.

Danny If there's anything I can do –

Lisa There's nothing.

Danny You'll tell me –

Lisa How about we move to another city? Or another planet?

Danny Lisa, I . . .

Lisa There's nothing, Danny. Don't feel bad about it. It's just how it is.

The approaching protestors get louder. Lisa and Danny stand with their signs, look towards the noise.

SCENE FOUR
FRACTURES

The shop. Eve stands in the staff room, the rota on the desk behind her. The staff enter minus Bryn. Theresa and Steph are talking and laughing. Ismael is wearing one shoe, shaking the other upside down. Gabi is showing Faisa a pop video on her phone, both of them dancing. Paul sits in one chair, then another, watching Faisa.

Eve Right, we've got twenty minutes. Let's use them.

Theresa Where's Alan?

Eve Garston. He sends his apologies.

Paul Bryn's getting a Curly Wurly from the shop. He told me to say.

Theresa (*going to leave*) I thought we were having a staff meeting?

Eve We *are*.

Paul Or he might have a Crunchie. If there isn't a Curly Wurly.

Faisa (*approaching the desk*) Is this the rota?

Eve Leave it. Just for a sec.

Paul He gets low blood sugar, that's the thing.

Eve Alright, Paul.

Gabi (*trying to look at the rota*) That should've been up yesterday.

Eve This is what I want to talk about.

Theresa Don't say the rota's changing. I've got my Monday, Wednesday, Friday –

Faisa I've got college so my days are my days.

Gabi I can't switch with anyone. Just saying, straight off.

Bryn (*entering, eating a Curly Wurly*) What are we switching?

Gabi If I'm not here, I'm in the Spendwell so don't start talking 'bout switching.

Eve Can we all just breathe? It's like feeding time at the zoo in here.

They all look stop and look at her, questioning.

Look, it's not good news . . . Take's been low: we all know that.

Bryn Oh, Jesus in pyjamas . . .

Eve So just for now – just until things improve . . . There'll be cuts to hours.

Gabi How much?

Bryn How many hours?

Paul What's 'for now'? Like a week?

Eve A month. Until next month. I need to look at the staffing in more detail –

Theresa I need the Monday, Wednesday, Friday. The grandkids. I can't mess up the routine.

Bryn I saw this. I knew it. (*Of Eve.*) Her and him whispering, swapping glances . . .

Steph (*to Bryn*) Wind your neck in, Bryn. Eve's just explaining.

Theresa We'll take it to the union. Tell them we're getting shafted.

Eve The union'll have nothing to say – it's the contracts we signed.

Faisa I don't remember that.

Bryn (*to Eve*) How many hours've you got?

Eve Twenty-five.

Bryn That's all I'm on now. How've you wangled that?

Eve Have I ever messed you about? Any of you?

Bryn (*of Ismael*) How many's *he* gonna get?

Eve I don't know yet, I –

Bryn Cheap labour'll win the day though, eh?

Faisa (*to Bryn*) What did you call me?

Bryn I know you take less than I do.

Faisa My wages are nothing to do with you.

Bryn They're everything to do with me. I'm trying to pay for a shitting wedding here.

Gabi (*getting between them; to Bryn*) Dial it down, Bryn.

Bryn (*to Gabi*) Why? You on the same scab deal as him?

Theresa (*to Eve*) Thing is, I can't have the hours going up and down. The kids. I can't . . .

Eve This isn't me. Okay? None of this is me.

Faisa But it's you who needs to sort this out. You need to sort this out with *him*.

Steph You will though, won't you, Eve?

Bryn She's gonna do her nut.

All turn and look at him.

A year planning the bloody thing – I'm gonna tell her we can't afford it. She's gonna do her bloody *nut*.

Lights down.

SCENE FIVE
DAWN LIGHT

Eve's front room. Iris sits with a plate of beans on toast on her lap. Eve stands.

Iris You don't have to stay. I will eat it, you know?

Eve I won't be long in the shops. There's a new box of tea bags under the sink; don't start ransacking the place looking for them.

Iris I'm not an idiot.

Eve Did I say you were?

Iris No one says it, everyone thinks it. That Danny's the worst.

Eve What's he supposed to've done now?

Iris Ever since all that fuss in the newsagent's –

Eve Mum –

Iris I mix up a few receipts and it's the end of the world.

Eve Mum, we're not talking about that.

Iris Ten years I put in there. I short change a few people, I'm out the door.

Eve Will you eat something? For me?

Iris eats grudgingly.

Iris It's Lisa you should be worrying about, not me.

Eve Lisa's fine. She's fine, isn't she?

Iris She's not exactly chipper. You're not here – you don't see.

Eve She's fallen out with some of the other kids –

Iris A girl who keeps the curtains shut in the blazing sunshine is blocking something out.

Eve Don't know what's worse: her moping or Danny *smiling* all the time . . .

Iris Not surprised he's smiling – all he does is fiddle on that computer.

Eve It's the job-seeking isn't it?

Iris He needs to get out there with a nice tidy CV, knock on some doors.

Eve He needs to do thirty hours a week on this site or he won't get his dole.

Iris Seeking what?

Eve Anything. Everything. Yesterday he applied for head chef at the Panoramic.

Iris He'll never get that.

Eve (*sarcastic*) Do you think?

Iris Are these 'Value' beans? 'Cause some things aren't worth saving on –

Eve covers her face suddenly with a cry of frustration.

Evie? Don't be silly, love, what's up?

Eve What did you do when Dad lost his job, Mum?

Iris What did we *do*?

Eve You and him. How did you cope?

Iris We fought back. Out on the docks next day, front of the picket lines. All fuel to him.

Eve I'm not sleeping. I wake up fighting with things.

Iris You were always like that. Screaming in the night, telling me you could see spiders and gorillas – all kinds of made-up things.

Eve These aren't made-up things.

Iris (*looking out*) Those windows are getting filthy.

Eve What?

Iris The *windows*. Next door'll think we've turned heathen.

Eve Are you listening to me?

Iris The fella came round when you were out but I had to tell him to leave it. Nothing in the pot.

Eve There was ten quid. I put ten quid in there for the windows and the little shop.

Iris There was nothing in the pot.

Eve (*moving to look*) There was ten pound there, Mum.

Iris It's not worth getting upset about, pet –

Eve Where did it go?

Iris – a dirty window.

Eve Where did it go, Mum? *Think*.

Iris You'll have to ask your dad.

Eve What?

Iris He'll know better than I do. He looks after that sort of thing.

Eve What are you talking about?

Iris What's the face on *you* for?

Eve Dad's dead, Mum.

Beat.

He's ten foot under in Walton cemetery. So how can I ask him anything?

Iris I know he's dead. I know that.

Eve Then stop all that –

Iris (*nodding*) His heart . . . I know he's dead.

Eve Then stop talking nonsense.

Iris I know that.

Eve Could you just for a minute . . .

Eve turns away, beginning to cry, fighting it.

Iris Oh, Eve pet . . . What's all this?

Iris moves over to her, putting her arms around her, shushing her.

Eve I need you to really try and listen to me, Mum.

Iris What? Listen to what?

Beat. Eve tries to find the words.

I gave it to the man.

Eve What man?

Iris That ten pound. I gave it to the man who came to the door. He was collecting for the sick kiddies.

Eve Course you did.

Iris You've got to help if you can, haven't you?

Eve I'm going to sort things out for you, Mum. I'm going to take care of it.

Iris Don't be silly. Nothing's needs sorting.

Eve I'm going to work everything out.

Iris Everything's fine, pet. Everything's just right . . .

They stay like this for some moments. Iris moves away.

Eve (*sung*)
My level head, my steady hand
My place between the sky and land
The ground that lies beneath my feet
Is up in flames, is spinning free

Chorus.

Come lift me up, come hold me tight
Chase away the circling night

Say soft and sweet, 'It'll be alright.
We'll be bold and brave in the new dawn light.'

If I'm standing straight
If I'm breathing strong
If I keep the faith
Will I soldier on?
The skyline slides into the sea
Brick and stone blown on the breeze

Repeat chorus.

Eve watches Iris.

Come lift me me up, come hold me tight . . .

Lights down.

SCENE SIX
MAGICAL TIMES

Lisa sits on the step of the house with her coat on. She stands as she sees Eve approaching.

Lisa Before you start making a mountain –

Eve What? Tell me what I'm gonna say.

Lisa That I'm stupid.

Eve Wrong.

Lisa That I'm ruining my chances.

Eve Keep talking.

Lisa Everyone else gets to act up sometimes. The second I do anything, everyone loses their mind.

Eve I've just been talking to a very upset science teacher. He wants me to take you to a counsellor.

Lisa He's only scared my marks'll drop and I'll mess up his average.

Eve What's this about you eating your lunch in the toilets?

Lisa I've got to eat it somewhere.

Eve He reckons you've got some kind of disorder.

Lisa I can't have them all watching and laughing. If it's egg sandwich they make fart noises, if it's tuna they say I stink. If it's a 'Value' yoghurt – that's the best one –

Eve Who's this?

Lisa Taking pictures of me with me mouth full – sticking them on Instagram.

Eve You tell me who.

Lisa I didn't mean to upset Mr Wan. They were all going on like always. I just wanted . . . just . . .

Eve Just what? (*Beat.*) What, tell me . . . Pet –

Lisa I just thought if I could do something mad – like something funny and brave and not like me, I could shock them all, I could get them talking about something else.

Eve So you wrote an obscenity on the board?

Lisa It was a formula. If the wavelength of light is ten angstroms the frequency equals . . .

Eve Equals what?

Lisa He always makes me get up in front of everyone. All of them shouting: 'Lisa'll do it.' 'Lisa always gets it right.' And I thought 'What if I don't? What if this time the frequency of light equals . . .'

Eve Equals?

Lisa 'Prick off Mr Wan.'

Beat. Eve looks at her in confusion.

I don't know – I panicked.

Eve 'Prick off'? Is that even a thing?

Lisa Tilly Banner wrote 'Fuck you' on the board last week and everyone thought it was amazing. But 'cause it's me – 'cause it's still me, it's always me . . .

Eve What do you mean 'still' you? I don't want you to be anything but you.

Lisa You're the only one.

Eve I'll go in and talk to the head. She'll sort these kids out –

Lisa (*shaking her head*) I can't be doing it, Mum. I'm not doing it any more.

Eve Don't talk silly.

Lisa All of them staring at me.

Eve You're a year and a bit off your exams.

Lisa Talking 'bout me, texting each other and laughing.

Eve You'll go to sixth form – all the divvies'll drop out.

Lisa You think I'm messing. I can't do it.

Eve As if you're gonna throw everything away over –

Lisa What am I throwing away?

Eve Your science, your studying.

Lisa My science? You don't know anything about it.

Eve You know what he called you?

Lisa What world do you live in?

Eve He said 'extraordinary'. He used that word. He said 'Your daughter is –'

Lisa I don't *want* to be extraordinary. What good does it do me, not being ordinary?

Eve He said he's never had a student like you.

Lisa So I'm dancing off to uni, am I? Getting on a train to London or Glasgow? Nan's losing her fucking mind.

Eve Don't speak to me like that.

Lisa She locked herself in the yard again yesterday. You know that? I found her trying to climb the wall like a cat.

Eve Don't worry about that – I'll worry about that.

Lisa She needs looking after.

Eve So I'll look after her.

Lisa You'll jack in the job?

Eve If it gets to that.

Lisa Then who's gonna work? Who's bringing money in?

Suddenly she hugs her tightly.

Eve Oh Lis . . . I'm sorry . . .

Lisa pulls away.

Lisa I'm not some dozy kid, always in a daydream –

Eve Who said you were?

Lisa I hear you and Danny – on about the rent and the bills. You want me to pretend I don't?

Eve I just want you to be yourself. Like before, like in juniors.

Lisa *Juniors?* I see how things are. I can *see*.

Eve I see you . . . and you're . . . the cleverest person I've ever met. And these kids –

Lisa Why are we all walking round like everything's alright?

Eve It will be. It *will* –

Lisa You can't tell me that everything's alright.

Lights down. Eve moves away. The band plays 'Magical Times'. In the shop Bryn is taking garden ornaments out of a trolley, arranging them. He slips, hurting his finger – loses it suddenly, kicking the ornaments, smashing them one by one. He stops at last, stands breathless in the debris. Lights down on Bryn. Elsewhere Danny is flyering 'Remain' leaflets.

Lisa (*sung*)
These are magical times, rootless and wild
We are dancing unbound, unruled by the tides
I see ghosts of stars in a rolling sky
These are magical times, and where am I?

These are wondrous days when planets align
Sun and moon kiss and the dark swallows fire
I see silver and gold scattered high and wide
These are magical times, and where am I?

There are men singing songs from space
And I'm gravity, I'm endless weight
I saw the sky alight, too late
A million years ago
A million miles away
These are magical times, and where am I?

A great wind blows through, scattering Danny's flyers from his hands. He stares bewildered.

SCENE SEVEN
NEGOTIATIONS

The shop, afternoon. Faisa sticks 'Sale' labels to items. Voice over tannoy: 'Fancy a garden party? Our super hot summer sale is now on: massive reductions on albarbecues and decking. Top brands at tiny prices.' Eve sits on the back step holding a lit cigarette. Steph approaches fast, making Eve jump.

Steph Sneaky bitch. (*Grabbing the cigarette.*) You with a fag: it's like 1995 all over again.

Eve Found it in a drawer in the office. Probably one of yours.

Steph Wait till I tell your Danny.

Eve Tell Danny what you like – just don't tell Lisa.

Steph laughs, sits, taking a drag.

Steph Remember Sister Mary Michael caught you smoking by the ice-cream van?

Eve I remember you legged it and left me to her.

Steph It's not my fault you're a slow-arse.

Eve She made me do a speech in mass. 'Why tobacco offends Jesus.'

Steph laughs. Eve takes the cigarette back, takes a drag

Steph You heard 'bout Bryn's girlfriend? Binned him.

Eve You're joking? Teak-tan Tina?

Steph She's taking her tan elsewhere. He had some kind of breakdown in here yesterday. Details are murky but it involved two dozen clay tortoises and a selection of garden gnomes.

Eve I bet Alan was tearing his hair out.

Steph (*taking the cigarette back*) Let's hope so.

Eve He's not the enemy, Steph.

Steph He's doing a good impression.

Eve I know he comes across a bit . . . robotic.

Steph R2-D2's a bit robotic.

Eve He's trying, alright?

Steph Maybe he could try talking to the dole for me?

Eve Why, what did they say?

Steph A month. And if I get over sixteen hours a week in the meantime they'll cancel the claim. I can't stick that, Eve –

Eve Couple more weeks we'll be back to normal in here.

Steph You believe that? Why, 'cause he says so?

Eve If this place falls apart he's going with it. You saw how he was over his dad –

Steph His old fella died a year ago. Is he still milking that in your private moments?

Eve (*pulling the cigarette off Steph*) Shut up, you.

Steph At least when his dad was in charge we had a laugh round here.

Eve I'll pass that on, shall I? 'Steph's not having enough fun. She needs more time for pissing about'?

Steph Eh?!

Eve You'd have a laugh in a mortuary.

Inside, Theresa pushes her cleaning trolley quickly across the floor, Alan following.

Alan They can't be here, Theresa. It's the law. It's all kinds of laws.

Theresa *I* shouldn't be here.

Eve (*to Steph*) Hang on . . .

Theresa You text me last night to come in today –

Eve and Steph move inside during the following, listening.

Alan I can't have two babies toddling round my office.

Theresa They're six and four.

Alan There are Health and Safety implications. Child protection.

Theresa I'm never here Tuesday. You've got me ringing round my whole family –

Eve and Steph approach.

Alan Where's your Anna?

Theresa You tell me. I've had two phone calls since Christmas.

Alan Look, Theresa, I understand it's not ideal.

Steph I'll take them.

Alan Take them where? You're in here till five.

Eve Al, seriously: weigh up your options.

Steph (*to Theresa*) You could've rung me. What's wrong with you?

Theresa You've got three of your own.

Steph What's two more? The carpets are already ruined.

A crash and a child's scream followed by child's laughter from off.

Alan (*to Steph and Theresa*) Just get those children out of my office.

Theresa and Steph hurry off towards the noise.

(*To Eve.*) Is there some kind of conspiracy? Bring the place down from the inside?

Eve I spent half an hour calming Faisa down this morning.

Alan *Everyone* needs to calm down.

Eve She's got credit cards, student loan, the bloody catalogue.

Alan Thanks for dealing with her.

Eve I don't need thanking, I need information. People need to plan.

Alan I'd love to know the plan.

Eve We said a month – we're halfway there.

Alan Right now I'm trying to see past a shower of shit.

Eve (*pulling him aside*) I'm dangerously close to lying to people here, Al.

Alan Just bear with me, alright? Brexit's spooked the shareholders – everything's up in the air.

Eve Should I be looking for something else?

Alan *No*. No, don't do that to me.

Eve To you?

Alan I need you here.

Eve Danny's lost his job. No redundancy. My mum's missing in action.

Alan What d'you mean?

Eve She's talking her own language half the time.

Alan (*taking her hand*) Christ, Eve . . .

Eve What do I do? Play along with her nonsense? Look her in the eye and tell her she's going mad?

Alan Got to a point with my dad, I just let him believe what he believed. You nod, you smile . . .

Eve Watch them leave the room while they're standing in front of you.

He nods. He hugs her.

Al, if things are changing round here . . . If you could put a word in for me upstairs . . . ? If you could try . . .

Alan Someone needs to put a word in for me.

Eve I mean, after all that at Christmas –

Alan What at Christmas?

Eve You said if there was ever anything you could do . . .

Alan I meant it. If there *was* anything I could do –

Eve I've only ever worked for you or your dad. I've worked hard. Haven't I?

Alan Course you have, but you're not qualified, you're –

Eve When you took over, I held your hand every step.

Alan You helped. You did.

Eve Five years we've run this place together. You tell them. You *tell them that.*

Alan I can't tell them anything right now: they're not bloody listening.

Eve You took me aside at that party. You talked in my ear. You promised.

Alan I was drunk.

Eve 'You won't ever want for much with me around, Eve.'

Alan I don't know what I said.

Eve That's what you said.

Alan What did he do?

Beat. She looks at him in confusion.

To get himself sacked?

Eve Smashed up a van. They said he was speeding.

Alan There are options in life, Eve. There always are. If you stick with someone who can't take care of you or your kid – if you carry on complaining while nothing's changing, aren't they just the choices you're making? (*Beat.*) I wish I could help you.

SCENE EIGHT
ZERO HOUR BLUES

Night. The band plays 'Zero Hour Blues'. Eve enters her bedroom carrying a box. She sits on the bed, removing items. In the living room Lisa lies on the couch under a duvet, watching a documentary about space. Iris sits in the dark kitchen, watching and listening tensely. Alan is in the shop at his desk, staring ahead. The rest of the staff are each at home unable to sleep.

Eve 'Child's wellies. Red. Child size 12. Used. Current bid: £3.' 'Blue sun dress with floral pattern. Size 12. Current bid £6.60.' 'Gorgeous imitation pearl stud earrings. Winning bid: 99p.' 'Vintage 60s tea set. Winning bid: £8.99'. £3 + £6.60 + 99p + £8.99 = £19.58 minus 70p in seller fees = £18.88. (*Beat.*) £18.88 for

Lisa's wellies from when she was six that she wrote her name in and wore even in bed. For the dress I had on when Danny took me to Southport beach and the weather was so bad we got wind burn. For the earrings he bought me when we were nineteen and he told me one day he'd afford the real thing. For my mum's china tea set I used to play with and pretend I was the Queen. All those precious things lined up, listed – categorised and washed out by the flash: a lifetime. A mountain of junk. Of treasured tat. All the things that made me and all the things I'm made of: worthless.

Steph (*sung*)

I heard things are looking up
God is in his heaven
And the stars are lining up
Tie my hair with white heather
Cross my fingers tight
Burn me a candle through the sleepless night
I'll wish on the waxing moon
I've got the zero hour blues

I'll keep in line, I'll keep the rules
Keep good time, I'll be anyone's fool
I'll be hanging on the line
For a drop of gratitude
For a better day to find me

Steph/The Staff (*sung*)

I'll sing to the waxing moon
I've got the zero hour blues

Nod once for yes and tap twice for luck
Dance for your supper and keep your chin up
Give me a note
And I'll sing to your tune
And hope you recognise it

Steph/The Staff
I'll howl to the waxing moon
I've got the zero hour blues

As the song ends lights focus on Eve. Danny enters, improvises a trumpet-fanfare sound with his mouth, holding a bowl of bananas and custard with a candle burning in the top.

Danny Are you hungry?

Eve What exactly is *that*?

Danny *This* is finely sliced, slightly brown banana, smothered in custard *à la* tin from the most far-flung and exotic corner of our kitchen cupboard.

Eve You've been in the pub.

Danny And wait, wait for it . . .

He pulls a little tub of ice-cream sprinkles from his pocket, letting them fall on the dish.

Sprinkles!

Eve What's this fabulous feast in aid of?

Danny (*sitting beside her*) Not in aid . . . in *lieu*. In lieu of any past anniversary or Valentine's Days I might've missed. And also any future ones.

Eve (*blowing out the candle*) What a deal. I'm a lucky girl.

He offers her a spoonful. She takes it, eats, grimaces.

Danny Is it alright?

Eve It's amazing. Bloody gorgeous.

Danny Is it?

Eve No, it's a bowl of rotten fruit with Ambrosia on top.

I think I'm gonna vomit here.

Danny Alright, give it to me gently.

She flicks some food at him. He ducks, laughs. He kisses her.

Eve You stink of ale.

Danny Ran in to Pav in a proper state. He thinks he's gonna get bundled on the next plane home to Krakow.

Eve Poor sod.

Danny He had a smile on his face after two pints.

Eve And he was paying?

Danny My treat.

Eve You're full of treats, aren't you?

Danny That's what they say.

He kisses her. Lisa turns up the sound on the TV/laptop. Danny looks towards it.

You gonna make her go to sleep at some point?

Eve I've said she can stay home tomorrow.

Danny So she can spend more time with your mother?

Eve It's complicated. I'm handling it.

Danny Iris is teaching her to crochet, you know? Lisa doesn't need to get any more weird – she doesn't need to crochet.

Eve Found me mum under the bed earlier, scrambling round for a brooch.

Danny When did she lose it?

Eve 1978, as far as I can work out.

Danny Jesus.

Eve She's dropping off the edge, Danny.

Danny She still remembers to call me a no-mark twice a day – can't have lost all her marbles.

During the following, Iris finds a bread knife and the stub of a loaf of bread in the kitchen. She cuts the bread but then keeps cutting, sawing into the table.

Eve Psychiatric nurse came over today. Did all these little tests – 'What year is it, Iris? 'Can you hold a pencil steady?' Apparently she's got a critical or substantial need for care.

Danny Critical or substantial?

Eve She might get three free days a week in a centre. If a place comes up. If someone else pops it. And I could pay but that's ten pound a day plus three-fifty for lunch and ten pound for the minibus.

Danny Cuts, isn't it? Everywhere you look. Heartless bastards.

Eve And even then she'd be back here by four. I could apply for carer's allowance if I didn't work, but they'd only give me half what I earn now. And care homes – we can't begin to afford –

Danny (*going to her*) Aren't we getting ahead of ourselves?

Eve No we're not. We're getting behind. We're going under. One of these days I'm gonna come home and she'll be lying at the bottom of the stairs or the house'll be on fire.

Danny Nothing's going on fire, alright? We'll work it out.

Eve How? Tell me how, Dan.

During the following Lisa becomes aware of the sound from the kitchen, approaches Iris.

Danny Look, I didn't want you getting excited . . . I've got this thing the day after tomorrow – St George's Hall.

Eve What thing?

Danny Something to do with the council. It was just an email: 'You've got an interview. Turn up midday.'

Eve They said 'interview'?

Danny Listen, there's plenty more skint than we are. Pav's been selling off the furniture since his missus left.

In the kitchen Lisa sees Iris with the knife, approaches quickly.

Lisa (*grabbing her arm*) Nan?

Iris screams in fright, brandishing the knife at Lisa.

Danny (*jumping up off the bed*) Jesus!

Eve (*jumping up*) Mum?!

Lisa (*to Iris*) Nan, it's me. It's *me.*

Lisa tries to take the knife but Iris shoves her away, staring, wild. Danny and Eve approach.

Eve (*going to them*) Mum, what are you doing?

Danny tries to intervene but Eve pushes him aside, going to Iris.

Mum. Mum, it's alright. (*Of the knife.*) Give me that.

Iris What's she doing? What the hell's she doing?

Eve She's not doing anything, Mum.

Iris Sneaking around the house. What about little Lisa?

Eve (*taking the knife*) This *is* Lisa, Mum.

Iris looks at Lisa sharply.

Eve Look at her. *This* is Lisa.

Iris stares in confusion, as if looking in a distorting mirror. She shakes her head.

Iris I don't . . .

Lisa It's me, Nan.

Iris I took the day off work when Lisa was born – I said to the boss: 'I can't be messing round here. I've got a baby to meet.'

Lisa I'm not a baby any more, Nan.

Eve You were dreaming, Mum. Imagining things.

Iris (*nodding*) I was dreaming. It was a dream.

Danny (*putting his arm round Iris*) How about you get to bed eh, Iris?

She shifts away, startled and wild again.

Eve (*hugging Iris*) Leave her. (*To Iris.*) It's alright. It's all alright.

Iris I was dreaming. It's only a dream.

Lisa and Danny look on.

It was only dreaming.

Danny turns, exits. Lisa looks to him for comfort, watches him go. Iris moves away from Eve, looking out, searching for something. Lights down on everyone but Iris.

Iris (*sung*)
I've been sleeping with the dead
I've been watching their shapes in my bed
The things I think I thought I was
Carried away with the wind on the rock
I'm sand
I'm sand

I've been beating my retreat
I've been burying my most precious things
In the garden in the flower bed
My blindest thoughts, my things unsaid
I'm soil
I'm soil

I remember every thud
Every name of everyone I ever loved
My heart's still beating through the mud
Don't know who you are
I know I should

Chorus.

Storm's coming over I've fallen in love
With what's left of me
The rest of me
Storm's coming over I've fallen in love
With what's left of me
The rest of me
Throw it to the dogs
Throw me to the gods

Think of me now I'm losing slowly
The thing about me now is I'm losing slowly
Strange children talk to me I'm losing slowly
The better part of me moving slowly away
I'm sand
Moving slowly away
I'm sand

Repeat chorus. Music continues. Lisa approaches, watching her.

Iris (*turning*) Jimmy . . .?

Iris smiles at Lisa, puts out her hand. Lisa approaches, taking it. They dance a waltz, Iris elated. Lights down.

SCENE NINE
CLOSURE

The band plays 'Whole Again'. The staff approach the shop to discover it closed up. Perhaps sheets have been thrown over everything, a closure notice pinned up. Faisa takes the notice, reads it in disbelief. They all stand and stare.

The Staff (*sung*)
One of these days I'm gonna rant and rail
One of these days I'll be whole again (*Repeat.*)

I tell you I reached the bottom and reached for the top
Kicked off the sand and I swam for the rocks
I saw the high sweet horizon and the sun gold hot
And it was slipping through my fingers like an old silk cloth

One of these days I'm gonna rant and rail
One of these days I'll be whole again (*Repeat.*)

I climbed a mountain just to see down town
Where they're turning the money, grinding smiles out of frowns
I worked for days and years to make a life's work pay
And watched them dash it all down the wall again

These days . . . these days . . .
One of these days I'm gonna rant and rail
One of these days I'll be whole again

Steph, Theresa and Faisa exit, still singing. The song dies out as Bryn and Ismael move in different directions. Paul stands absolutely still, staring at the shop. Gabi goes to him.

Gabi You getting the bus home?

Paul I can't go home . . . She'll say it's my fault.

Gabi Who will?

Paul Three years it took me to get in here. I'd get interviews and interviews and if I could just *talk to people*, just know the right and wrong words . . . That's what Mum says. (*He begins to stutter as he speaks.*) I've got A-levels you know, I . . . ?

Gabi You're talking to me now.

Paul Not really. I'm more talking at you.

Gabi It's a start.

Paul I've had lots of things to say. To you. On different days. Lots of times I wanted to . . .

Gabi You want to go to a pub?

Paul I have been to a pub. Me and my mum did the Toby Carvery once –

Gabi I mean with me now.

Paul Really?

Gabi No, I'm being sarcastic.

Paul (*turning away*) Oh, okay . . .

Gabi Paul . . .

She holds out her hand. He takes it.

Paul I like your eyes.

Gabi (*leading him off*) Did your mum tell you to say that?

Paul No. (*Beat.*) Well, yeah. But it's true . . .

Gabi smiles. They exit. Bryn approaches Ismael. Ismael holds his watch up to the light.

Bryn Hey mate . . . nice watch.

Ismael glares at him, turns and walks away.

It won't make a difference, will it?

Ismael stops and looks at him.

All this stuff lately. It won't change anything? (*Beat.*) I was in the pub, night after the vote came in, and all these fellas were shouting, and singing: 'Rule Britannia'. And I've never liked that tune and I don't know why anyone needs to rule waves, but just then it felt good to sing about ruling something – like something was happening, like something must be happening if everyone believed it – like something must've bust open. But it hadn't, had it?

Faisa No. No, I don't think so.

Bryn Nothing's changing, is it? Not for us.

Faisa So it's 'us' now?

Ismael starts to walk away. Bryn follows.

Bryn You haven't got a sofa I could kip on? Just a day or two. My girl kicked me out.

Faisa Why would you want to sleep on the sofa of a scab?

Bryn That was only talk, mate – you know the way I talk.

Faisa I never took anyone's work. I never took anyone's money.

Bryn I was just pissed off.

Faisa So now I'm pissed off. So piss off.

Ismael exits. Bryn looks after him hopelessly.

SCENE TEN
A PROPOSAL

In darkness we hear Eve banging on metal shutters, yelling from outside.

Eve (*outside*) A text message?! A fucking text message, Alan?!

Lights up on Alan sitting at his desk in the semi-darkness of the boarded-up shop. He rises, moves towards the noise as a door opens and slams and Eve staggers in.

(*Gesturing around.*) Is this it, then? Board us up and pack us away? Not even a closing-down sale?

Alan Nothing's ours to sell. We've been absorbed.

Eve Is that right?

Alan The stock, the capital, the assets such as they are –

Eve Five years running round after you making your mistakes look passable, tidying up your crumby little business –

Alan It happened overnight.

Eve You sneak behind my back and shut the place on my day off.

Alan I got a phone call. That was it.

Eve You could've rung me. You could've told me –

Alan *I couldn't bear to say the words.*

Eve You saw this coming.

Alan If I saw it you saw it, Eve.

Eve I asked you *straight* –

Alan My dad never let a single person go. Started with a staff of ten, finished with two hundred. That was his pride.

Eve You couldn't bear to fall so you drag the rest of us through the muck.

Alan The day he opened the second shop in Aintree . . . Standing there grinning in the middle of the industrial estate like he'd discovered the new world. He said to me, 'We were shopkeepers, kid. Now we're businessmen.' He had no bloody idea.

Eve You pinned a note to the door, Al.

Alan The further you climb the smaller you feel. The further you look up, the more you see there's something unreachable, untouchable . . . These men and their money. You think I'm the man with the money – you've got no idea.

Eve A note on the door.

Alan Would it'd've felt any better if I'd rounded them up and given them a hug? It's all the same, it's all done. I've got nothing.

Eve If you've got nothing, where does that leave the rest of us?

Alan He never knew I'd signed everything away. He was doolally by then. He thought he'd left me an empire.

Eve I didn't come here to talk about you, Al.

Alan We had each other and we had the business. Me and him. It's all gone.

He crumples, tears in his eyes. Beat. She goes to him. He takes her hand.

You're kind to me, Eve . . . People aren't any good really – you see that in business.

Eve Maybe you need to meet some new people.

Alan You're good.

Eve Good doesn't pay the bills though, eh?

Alan The directors offered me a job out in Cheshire: management consultancy. Corporate nightmare, but I'll have to take it –

Eve pulls her hand away sharply.

Hang on, I'm trying to say something –

Eve *You're* the one with no idea. No idea what it means to lose.

She turns to go quickly but he follows.

Alan Don't, don't go . . .

Eve I'll see you around.

Alan You won't though, will you?

Beat. She turns and looks at him.

Stay with me.

Eve What?

Alan I've got space to spare. Good area. Good schools. You and Lisa and your mother . . .

Eve Don't be stupid.

Alan What's stupid? You wanted me to help: this is how I can help.

Eve And Danny? You'll help him too?

Alan I've seen you. I've seen the days when you're heavy on your feet and the days when the shadows are under your eyes. I've been watching it for years and *always* I've thought to myself: 'She deserves more.' (*Beat.*) You deserve more, Eve . . . You know that, don't you?

Eve It's just lately. It's just a bad bit of luck.

Alan You want to look after your daughter, your mother? Think of what you're doing with your life. Think what you're doing to them –

Eve Don't you dare –

Alan No, I will, I will. Because some things we *can* control –

She stares at him.

Can't this be simple? Can't this be my gift to you?

Lights down.

SCENE ELEVEN
WHY HAVE IT HARD?

The band plays 'Why Have it Hard?'. Evening. Eve enters her house and begins to tidy the kitchen frantically. Iris is in the yard digging up dahlias, re-planting, perplexed, muttering. Lisa is in the living room with curtains closed, headphones on, reading a book. Eve stops suddenly, exhausted, leans on the table.

Alan (*sung*)
There's a gentle path that softly thins
There's an open door banging in the wind
There's a simple song for us to sing
Does it make me weak to want it?

Chorus.

Why have it hard, love? Why take it so
Rough, why can't you know
There are answers to all of these questions?
Why have it hard?

There's a sleepy end to this wild parade
Tie the streamers up, pack the band away
There's music where the quiet plays
And does it make you weak to want it?

Repeat chorus.

Alan (*sung*)
And my heart is the loudest drum
And my hopes are oceans crashing
And my arms are open, asking
Why have it hard?
Why have it hard?

Iris watches the flowers, waiting for them to grow. Danny enters, goes to Eve, hugs her. She turns to look at him, smiles. Lights down as the song ends, replaced by sparse percussion.

SCENE TWELVE
ONE DAY I WANT TO GET STRAIGHT

Food bank. The band continues the rhythm as Steph, Theresa, Gabi and Faisa move through the set, picking up tins, packets of dried food etc. Eve is alone elsewhere clutching bills, bank statements.

Eve (*staring out*) Deficit of £117.89 minus £18.88 equals . . . £99.1 pence. Cuts . . . cuts . . . (*Looking through papers.*) The phone, the laptop . . .? Direct debits already gone. Rent's due on Friday. Cuts . . . cuts . . . £177.63 minus £99.01 = £78.62. (*Beat.*) £78.62 for food this month, £19.65 for food this week . . . 4 pounds and 91 pence *each* for food this week . . .

Faisa (*sung*)
One day I wanna get straight
One day I wanna get straight
I'm not asking for riches
Or an overflowing plate
But one day I wanna get straight

I've been working for the money
For the money I owe
And it's taking the best part of me
I've been sleeping with the worry
Of the money I owe
It's talking through the small hours to me

Faisa/ Steph/ Theresa/ Gabi (*repeat chorus*)
One day I wanna . . .

Faisa (*sung*)
Come take me, take me
To another old town
Where no one knows my name
Where the wind won't blow sharp
In the winter time
And I'm new with each new day

Faisa/ Steph/ Theresa/ Gabi (*sung*)
One day I wanna get straight
One day I wanna get straight
I'm not asking for riches
Or an overflowing plate
But one day I wanna
One day I'm gonna
One day I wanna get straight

Eve looks around at the stacks of food, overwhelmed. Steph crosses with a box of tins, wearing a volunteer's uniform. Seeing her, Eve turns sharply to leave.

Steph *Eve . . .?*

Eve turns to her, forces a smile.

You blanking me now?

Eve You working here?

Steph Volunteering. Could do without it today – I'm cream-crackered.

Eve (*looking round*) The kids been playing up again?

Steph (*shaking her head*) Started last night in this office in town. Six hours cleaning on me tod. I was talking to the Henry Hoover by the end of it.

Eve I meant to ring you back this week – my mum's been all over the place.

Steph Don't stress, love, I know how it goes.

Eve (*turning*) I was just having a nose, so . . .

Steph You're here now – where's your voucher?

Eve My what?

Steph From the Job Centre – to prove you're in need.

Eve I'm not 'in need'.

Steph (*indicating others in earshot*) Don't let *them* hear that. (*Putting items in a box. Low.*) You like Angel Delight? Chickpeas?

Eve No. Actually *thanks*, but –

Steph Don't get embarrassed. It's only me.

Eve Who's embarrassed?

Steph (*packing food*) You know, if you're in a corner, me and the girls from the shop are gonna club together – start buying in bulk.

Eve What've I got to be embarrassed about?

Steph If you need any loo rolls, bar of soap . . .

Eve I've actually got some agency work lined up. Or I will have.

Steph And if you need someone for Iris, me and Theresa've got a rota going – for the kids –

Eve She's not a kid.

Steph Eve, you're not coping. You're losing weight –

Eve Who do you think you're talking to?

Steph You. Stood in front of me with handbags under your eyes.

Eve (*turning to go*) I know what you're doing.

Steph (*following*) Eve . . .? Do you want your food or not?

Eve Keep your voice down.

Steph (*shoving the box at her*) Who's listening?

Eve (*shoving it back, speaking low*) You were always the same. Ever since we were kids and you used to pull my skirt up in front of the boys.

Steph We were six. Are you not over that by now?

Eve Always been looking for every opportunity to give me a dig, knock me down a peg –

Steph Only when you needed it.

Eve Jealous. 'Cause I worked hard, 'cause I wanted something and everything wasn't just a laugh.

Steph Still got yourself pregnant by the biggest knobhead in the class, didn't you? *He* disappeared into a big puff of smoke – I wasn't too jealous of that.

Eve Fuck off, Steph.

Eve shoves the box at Steph as she moves away. It falls to the floor, tins rolling.

Steph You never thought maybe I was *proud* of you? Maybe I was proud to have a best mate like you. Maybe I'm alright with what I am and what I've got?

Eve stops and listens.

I've never been jealous. That was in your head. And what does that say about you, eh? What does that say about you?

Eve exits. Lights down.

SCENE THIRTEEN
CUTS

Eve sits on the floor bathed in the blue light of a laptop screen.

Eve £14 for a lipstick kiss + £20 for six used cotton buds + £25 for fingernail clippings with polish . . . Postmaster 3000 in London wants to me to lick a stamp and send it back to him: 20 quid . . . + £20 for ten eyelashes = £99. Everything's in demand somewhere. And in the corners of the net are the niche-est market places.

Eve takes a pair of scissors and begins to cut off her nails as she speaks.

There's girls on these sites selling pictures of themselves. No faces – just fragments, angles, selfies and mirror shots. £13 for a thigh + £18 for the whole leg + £28 for breasts + a tenner for the foot if that's your kind of thing + £40 for a fully body shot . . . £13 + £18 + £28 + £10 + £40 = £109. I could do a roast Sunday. I could buy Lisa some new clothes. (*Beat.*) John28 wants a private web chat. £200 quid and for that he wants every inch. Every detail. I could pay the credit card bill. Stop them ringing every day. (*Beat.*) £750 egg donation + £30 blood plasma

+ £40 blood platelets = £820. Egg donation every month, plasma every 48 hours, platelets every two weeks = £15,500 a year. £7,000 to rent a womb, £10,000 for a kidney= £17,000. Could go higher. Go further . . .

Eve closes her eyes, takes the scissors, takes a deep breath and slowly begins to cut off her hair. The music becomes discordant, chaotic as she cuts, hair falling. Music slows.

Eve (*sung*)
My weight in gold, in silver and lead
My diamond bones, my dreaming head
The price of me in black and red
I'm featherlight, I'm deficit

Chorus.

Come break me down, come crush me tight
My carbon eyes are burning bright
And the way you talk, it sounds so nice
But you'll comfort me with a smile and a knife

My hair, my clothes, my heart, my hope
The lines on my eyes and the letters I wrote
The sum of me in black and red
I'm feather light, I'm deficit

Repeat chorus. Lights down.

SCENE FOURTEEN
PERFECT

Night. Eve lies in bed, not asleep. Danny enters quietly in a crumpled cheap suit, no tie.

Eve How did it go?

Danny Go back to sleep.

Eve You think I've been asleep? Where've you been?

Danny Just walking. Round the park.

Eve What, in the dark? Like a pervert?

Danny Yeah, exactly like a pervert.

Eve How did it go?

Danny It didn't. Don't worry about it –

Eve But you got there alright?

Danny There'll be something else. Just don't get wound up.

Eve You were late, weren't you?

Danny Bloody hell, have a little bit of faith.

Eve I told you to leave loads of time.

Danny I was early. Bright eyed, bushy tailed, handsome and dazzling.

Eve Where's your tie? I told you to keep the tie on.

Danny Why'd you always think – ?

Eve You didn't wear the tie, did you?

Danny *I didn't mess it up.* (*Beat.*) I wore the tie. We all wore our ties. And our shiny shoes. Kids and old fellas and women in suits, 'bout a hundred of us all shuffling in to that great big shining hall . . . And they had all these stalls set out . . . Lists where you could sign up. Voluntary. Charities. Community groups . . . No one paying. The only one actually recruiting was the army.

Eve So why would they send you . . . ?

Danny 'Cause I went to a job interview today, didn't I? They get to tick that box and file that data and I've jumped through one more hoop . . . Wandering like an urchin asking: 'Who's got the jobs? Where are the jobs?' (*Beat.*) If Jimmy could've seen me today . . .

Eve (*taking his hand*) My dad took dole for ten years after they closed the docks. He had to. And he was never ashamed.

Danny I didn't mess it up.

Eve I know. I know.

She hugs him.

Danny It's not like I don't get it, Evie. I get it. Your mum, and Lisa's school and . . .

Eve And what?

Danny Thing is we've got to keep smiling somehow and if . . . if I can make you smile that's something I *can* do –

She kisses him. He pulls her to him. Beat. He draws back, squinting at her in the low light.

Danny What have you . . . ?

Eve What?

Danny (*sitting up*) What have you done?

Eve (*of her hair*) I cut it. Don't make a thing of it.

Danny All your hair, Evie . . .

Eve I wanted it short.

Danny It doesn't look like you.

Eve Well, it *is* me.

Danny Just like that? You cut it yourself?

Eve It's not that bad, is it?

Danny You *love* your hair.

Eve I love you. I love Lisa and my mum. Hair's just hair.

Danny What you talking like that for? *Evie?*

Eve I sold it.

Danny You what?

Eve Gabi told me about this site. Ten pound an ounce if it's in good condition.

Danny You *sold* it?

Eve Extensions. It's a big market now. Untreated hair's a premium.

Danny Are you messing about?

Eve I'll put it in the post – get seventy-five quid for the lot.

Danny You *sold* your hair?

Eve We're skint, Danny.

Danny We could've sold something else.

Eve Like what?

Danny You should've told me.

Eve You wouldn't have let me.

Danny That's why you should've told me.

Eve I went to the cash machine after work today. Thought I had twenty quid to get some shopping in. I'd planned it. It was there. And then I'm just staring at this machine, at these minus numbers and I'm trying to do the sum in my head. Because it must be one of the bills has gone up. It must be it's gone up and we've gone over and then they've fined us. And I feel like walking into the bank and calling them all thieves. But I'm just staring, and I realise there's a queue behind me and I must've been standing there for ages. And someone coughs. So I just walk away. I take my card and walk away. (*Beat.*) This sorts the fine. Puts us back to nothing.

Danny You didn't have to do that.

Eve I went round three admin agencies today. One glance at my CV, they look right through me. They want twenty-year-olds with business degrees to do the photocopying these days.

Danny I'll get my back pay any day now –

Eve Everything has to go on rent now, Danny – *everything*.

Danny You didn't have to.

Eve I had to do something.

He strokes her face, touches the edges of her hair.

Tell the truth: is it awful?

Danny You're perfect.

He kisses her.

Perfect . . . Perfect . . .

SCENE FIFTEEN
THE CRUNCH

The band plays off-kilter rhythms. In the bedroom Iris chases an invisible bird: batting at the air, bumping into things, increasingly determined. Lisa enters brushing her hair, watching Iris. In the kitchen Danny is making breakfast, Eve is searching through her handbag.

Danny Do you want toast?

Eve Lisa needs to eat something.

Danny I'm asking *you*.

Eve I've got to be at the Job Centre in half an hour.

Eve's phone rings in her bag. She digs for it, squints at the number, answers it.

Hello . . .

Danny Lisa! You want toast?

Lisa (*calling from upstairs*) Nan's chasing the budgie again.

Eve moves into the yard to escape the noise.

Iris (*making a jump for it*) There! The bastard . . .

Danny (*shouting up to her*) Iris! There's no bird, there never was a bird!

Iris Bloody bastard thing. It was Jimmy wanted it, not me. Always pecking and shitting on everything. (*Leaping in the air.*) There!

Eve looks to the noise. She turns away, talking quietly, urgently.

Danny Lisa?! Am I making you breakfast or not?

Lisa approaches, searching for her shoes. Iris continues to pursue the bird noisily.

(*Searching the kitchen.*) Where's the bloody . . . Eve, where's the toaster?!

Lisa She eBayed it. She's eBayed everything.

Danny Jesus. What we gonna eat now?

Lisa Bread. Obviously.

Upstairs Iris goes crashing into something.

Iris Stinking, shitting, squawking thing . . .

Lisa Someone'll have to catch it for her.

Danny There *is* no bird.

Lisa In *her* world there is.

Lisa finds her shoes while Danny butters bread and Iris stalks around after the bird.

Eve (*re-entering the kitchen*) Lisa, what you still doing here?

Lisa I'm going.

Eve Then go.

Lisa goes to the living room, searching for books, packing her bag, in no hurry. Iris makes another leap and falls over, yelling in frustration.

Danny (*shouting up*) Iris! I've caught the budgie! I've caught it and broken its bloody neck.

Iris sits slowly, taking this in, perturbed, muttering.

(*To Eve.*) Don't look at me like that: it's the only way to deal with her. (*Beat.*) Who was on the phone?

Eve stares at him.

Danny If it's the PPI tell them to piss off.

Eve It was the girl from the letting agency.

He turns to her sharply.

She said they need their money.

Danny No, I talked to her last week – I told her.

Eve She said the payment was two hundred short.

Danny They'll just have to wait for it.

Eve They've waited a week. It should've been there.

Danny Don't let her scare you. She's just putting the pressure on.

Eve Why wasn't it there?

Danny We've got rights here, Evie –

Eve *Why wasn't it there, Danny?*

Danny I lent it to Pav.

Eve You . . . ?

Danny It was *my* back pay, wasn't it?

Eve It was *our money*, it was *our rent*.

Danny He said it'd only be for a day, tide him over till his benefits came in.

Eve Then where is it?

Danny He missed a meeting or something: they sanctioned him.

Eve You gave it away?

Danny He'll pay me back.

Eve When? Now? Can I go round and get it now?

Danny He came here crying, Evie – you should've seen him. He's in bits with this bedroom tax business. They were gonna evict him –

Eve They're gonna evict *us*. They're gonna have us out. You put your mate before us?

Danny No. No, I'll talk to them again.

Eve *Why didn't you tell me?*

Beat.

Danny She said those words? She said 'evict us'?

Eve They've got new tenants lined up. They're 'initiating proceedings' –

Danny So we barricade the place. We've got rights, haven't we? If it comes to it we'll board up the door. Like the Kirkby rent strikes. Defend our property.

Eve It's not our property. We don't own any property.

Danny You've gotta fight, Evie –

Eve I've *been* fighting, Danny. Haven't you noticed? Haven't you seen me?

Danny (*approaching*) Evie . . . come on.

She shifts away from him.

Come on, worst case they throw us out – we'll get some advice, get a plan, kick back.

Eve What, dragging round charities and hostels and B & Bs?

Danny What did your dad used to say?

Eve Trapped in some mildewed room with my mum climbing the walls.

Danny Come on, say it like your dad used to: 'If we're breathing, if we're standing –'

Eve My dad's *dead*. Those words don't work any more.

Danny He died fighting.

Eve He died from the *stress*. From the fucking unfairness, the penny-pinching, the never-knowing-what's-coming – never safe, never safe. And I'm sorry, I can't live like that. I can't let Lisa live like that. It costs too much.

Danny You're safe. I keep you safe.

Eve I'm on my own.

Danny *I'm* here. I'm here and I love you.

Eve It's not enough.

Danny You love me.

Eve It's not enough.

Pause. Danny stares at her. In the living room Lisa has become aware of raised voices. She comes and listens outside the kitchen.

Eve Alan said he'd help us.

Danny What?

Eve Said we could stay with him.

Danny *Us?*

Eve Me . . . Me and Lisa and mum.

Danny *Jesus.* He . . .

Eve He'll get my mum looked after properly.

Danny *Alan?*

Eve I can't pretend there's nothing I can do, because there is. There *is*. Anything else is just a lie – a selfish lie.

Danny Are you sleeping with him?

Eve *No.*

Danny *Are you?*

Eve You *really* think that's what this is about?

Danny You're not going. I'm not letting you.

Eve It's not up to you.

Danny Lisa won't go – she won't want to go with you.

Eve She'll go to a new school. A better school. Like she needs. I *have* to.

Danny Stop saying that. If it's your choice, own up to it –

Lisa enters the kitchen, watching, unseen by them.

Eve It's *not* my choice.

Danny You're my Evie.

Eve We can't look after each other, Danny. What are we if we can't look after each other?

Danny I'll fix it.

Eve shakes her head

Danny I'll fix it.

Lisa Will you?

Eve and Danny turn sharply to see Lisa.

Go on then. Fix it. Magic it all better. What you gonna *do*, Danny?

Danny Lis . . .

Eve Go and pack a bag, love.

Lisa Danny?

Danny (*to Lisa*) You're my girl.

Eve When it suits you. When the going's good.

Danny (*to Eve*) That's my little girl.

Eve Ice creams and jokes and days out. You're good for that.

Danny I'm good for it all. I've raised that child.

Eve You gave away the rent, Danny. You gave away the roof over her head.

Danny (*to Lisa*) Have you heard her? Can you hear this mental shit she's talking?

He grabs Lisa's arm a bit too roughly. Lisa pulls away, startled.

Eve Lisa, pack a bag.

Lisa (*to Danny*) I'm sorry.

Eve *Lisa.*

Lisa looks from Danny to Eve. She exits to the living room, stands in shock.

Danny This is stupid. This is *us*, Evie. Just stay – you're gonna stay.

Eve I can't.

Danny (*going to her*) Stay with me.

Eve (*pushing him away*) Danny . . .

Danny You know what this makes you?

Eve I don't get to choose.

Danny Whoring yourself out . . .

Eve Don't say that word. You don't say that word.

Danny You *know* what this makes you.

Eve stares at him. Lights down.

SCENE SIXTEEN
TIME

The band plays 'Why Have it Hard?'. Eve, Lisa and Iris pack up items from their house. Iris and Lisa exit as Eve moves downstage. Lights shift. Eve sits in Alan's conservatory, sunlight on her face. A pot of food is nearby, a scarf is round her neck. She closes her eyes, breathes.

Eve Patent leather kitten-heel court shoes: £50. Two ultimate comfort T-shirt bras: £60, plus deep moisture skin balm: £35.50. Rich cotton button-down dress, £65. Rosti potatoes with lamb steak and goat's cheese starter, £45.75, plus tea for one with all-butter shortbread . . .

Music stops abruptly as Alan enters with briefcase. Eve jumps up, wiping the table, tidying.

Alan (*taking cloth from her*) Don't do that. I don't like that.

Eve What else am I doing all day?

Alan You haven't been out?

Eve I went into town.

Alan Only town?

Eve And the park.

Alan Your shoes are all muddy in the porch.

Eve I went round the park.

Alan On your own?

Eve On my own.

Alan (*indicating her scarf*) What's this . . . ? I haven't seen this.

Eve I'd had it years.

Alan Looks like you got it on the market.

Eve I did.

Alan (*taking it off her*) Wear that new one I got you – the pink one.

Eve Pink scarf: twenty-two pounds fifty.

Alan What?

Eve I'm keeping track of everything. Adding it all up. I'll pay you it all back.

Alan (*tasting the food in the pot*) You won't.

Eve Eventually.

Alan You followed the recipe?

Eve Could have something by next week. Asda want people on the tills.

Alan But that's not you, is it?

Eve If they'll have me. If I'm not under-qualified, I'm over-qualified . . .

Alan (*of the food*) Did you put spice in here?

Eve Only a bit.

Alan The recipe doesn't say spice.

Eve I thought it'd be nice.

Alan It *might* be nice but it's not the recipe.

Lisa enters upstage, dumps her school bag and books on the floor, moves quickly into another space in the house.

Eve (*calling through*) Alright, Lis?

Alan (*calling through*) You alright, love? School alright?

Beat. Lisa sighs.

Lisa Yep. One hundred per cent alright. Couldn't be more alright.

Alan nods and grins at Eve, giving her a thumbs-up. Eve forces a smile. Lisa puts in headphones and curls up in a chair. Alan squints at Lisa's bag and books.

Alan (*low to Eve*) Could you have a word with her maybe? About the stuff.

Eve The stuff?

Alan In the hall. On the floor in the hall. All the time. Only it's all the time.

Eve Sorry, I know she's –

Alan Don't say sorry. I don't want you to be sorry.

Eve I *am* sorry. I know we're in your way.

Alan Not in my way.

Eve We won't be here for ever.

Alan Did I say you were in my way? (*Going to her.*) This is your home, right? Both of you.

Eve That's kind, Al, but –

He moves to kiss her, she pulls away. She shakes her head. Pause.

Alan It's been a month.

Eve I know how long it's been.

Alan You've never been treated right – that's your problem. You don't how this is supposed to work.

Eve I haven't got a *problem*, Al.

Alan You like it here, don't you? You'd tell me if I was doing something wrong?

Eve You're not doing anything wrong.

Alan Let's go somewhere. You, me and Lisa. France or . . . Berlin. I hear Berlin's very cultural.

Eve We can talk about it.

Alan We're talking about it now.

Eve I'll have a think –

Alan A whole month, Eve . . . You've had time.

SCENE SEVENTEEN
EVICTION

Danny stands in the living room of his house. As he sings, the furniture is removed around him, repossessed. Elsewhere, Lisa looks at the stars through a telescope.

Danny (*sung*)
Where are all the drunken poets
Singing to the moonless night?

Where's your heart, where's your compassion
Where's your sharp unflinching sight?

I can feel your pulse, your rhythm
I can hear the notes are right
You'll tell me all my hopes are flashes
And call yourself a guiding light
But where's your soul?
Where's your soul?

Where's your roar and where's your spirit?
Where's your faith in the last good fight?
Come to me with heart on fire
Come with unextinguished light
Where's your soul?
Where's your soul?

Paul enters, looking round for Gabi. She runs after him, grabs him. He laughs. They kiss: a silhouette of young love, like Eve and Danny many years earlier.

Danny (*sung*)
I've got nothing left to give
But the gentlest of things
A gift I cannot bottle
Or tie up with string
My soul
There's my soul

Lights down. Gabi and Paul exit hand in hand. Danny stares out.

SCENE EIGHTEEN
HOME

Care home. Iris sits in an armchair. Eve sits beside her.

Iris She'll be here again in a minute, you watch, she'll be up there watching . . .

Eve There's no one there, Mum, I promise.

Iris You'll see, you'll see. (*Muttered.*) Thinks I'm stupid . . . Everyone thinks I'm stupid . . .

Eve This is a good place. I've told you that, haven't I?

Iris I know. I know what's going on.

Eve How about I do you a dinner at the weekend. In Alan's. Big piece of salmon – you'll like that?

Iris No one listens. Don't know why I bother.

Eve We'll sit in the garden after – sit and look and the flowers with nothing to worry about.

Iris You'll see, just watch. Keeps coming past that door –

Eve Mum . . . Did you love my dad?

Iris Wrong question.

Eve I mean, does it have to be that?

Iris 'Do you love me? Do you not?' Blah-di-blah. So I go round town with my mates? So I go out sometimes without telling him where?

Eve What's the right question?

Iris The second I had anything of my own, the second I did anything just for me and nothing to do with him, that question: 'Do you love me? Do you love me?' Course I loved him but there's got to be something else. There've got to be better bloody questions. (*Beat.*) You give everything away . . . (*Looking at Eve.*) You give everything away, Evie, just like me.

Eve takes Iris's hand. Iris leans forward suddenly, pointing.

There! There she is. She's staring at me.

Eve It's a nurse.

Iris What does she want? What's she doing?

Eve She's not doing anything: look.

Iris Go away! (*To Eve.*) Make her go away!

Eve She's here to look after you. They're all here to look after you.

Iris (*shaking her head, beginning to cry*) No one listens to me. No one listens. No one . . .

Eve (*putting her arms around her*) Look, she's gone, okay, Mum? She's gone.

Eve rocks her. Iris calms slowly, strokes Eve's hair.

Iris It was such a shame.

Eve What was?

Iris Such a clever girl. Such a whizz with numbers. Got up the duff by the first lad who winked at you – threw it all away.

Eve What?

Iris And then that Danny Scott – he never lit up the sky. You could have gone anywhere. Could have had anyone. You ended up with Danny bloody Scott from down the road.

Eve I wanted Danny Scott from down the road.

Iris (*whispered*) They pretend to help me, but they lock the doors.

Eve What should I have wanted?

Iris looks at Eve suddenly and smiles.

Iris When are we going home, pet? (*Beat.*) When can we go home?

Lights down.

SCENE NINETEEN
DUST

Evening. Alan's house. Lisa looks through a window with a telescope, surveying the sky. At intervals she makes notes. Eve enters and throws down a pair of boots. Lisa looks up.

Eve I got them for you. Forty minutes wandering round that shop like Mrs No Mates.

Lisa Who was?

Eve Me. Your mother. The one standing in front of you on Planet Earth.

Lisa Sorry . . . Crap. I was in science club, then –

Eve (*of the boots*) You said you wanted them.

Lisa *You* said I wanted them. I said nothing.

Eve So I'll take them back, shall I?

Lisa If it makes you happy.

Eve No it *doesn't* make me happy, Lisa.

Lisa squints at her in confusion, turns back to her telescope. Eve goes to leave, then turns.

You know, this doesn't cut it. This self-righteous act. Sneering at this place, this house –

Lisa Mum, I'm sorry I forgot about the shops.

Eve You think you're so real and so honest.

Lisa I don't think anything.

Eve Don't try and tell me you're not better off, alright? Don't tell me you're not happier in that nice private school with the lawns and the flowers everywhere –

Lisa I'll wear the boots. I like the boots.

Eve Don't try and tell me you don't like takeaway on a Saturday and roast on a Sunday. All your extra tuition. And that telescope: you know how much that cost?

Lisa Loads.

Eve I don't even know. Alan just bought it.

Lisa Course I like it.

Eve He just bought it.

Lisa Why you even asking me that?

Eve 'Cause you're never satisfied, Lisa.

Lisa What do you want me to say? The school's different, the kids are different but *I'm* not different. Everyone used to call me posh, now everyone thinks I'm common. People never used to leave me alone, now no one talks to me at all.

Eve Whatever clothes you need to fit in, whatever the other kids've got –

Lisa You can't buy the answer, Mum. Throw whatever money you like at it, I'm still me. And you're still you . . . And what are we doing here? How the hell did we get here?

Eve It's for you. Every bit of it's for you.

Lisa I know. That's the worst part.

Eve I know you miss Danny. I know it's hard.

Lisa Do *you* miss him?

Eve I'm giving you everything I never had. I'm giving you every chance.

Lisa It's not worth it.

Eve You might not know the worth of it now –

Lisa You remember when we all used to go the protests? When I was little. And you'd have the megaphone – screaming at the top of your lungs and everyone else screaming back. And people'd be looking out of cars and shop windows –

Eve And what did it change? All that screaming?

Lisa I was proud of you. You were . . . lit up.

Eve It's you I care about, Lisa. Not the crowd: you.

Lisa And it's *you* I care about, and I'm saying it's not worth it.

Beat. Lisa looks through the telescope again. Eve watches her.

Eve What are you looking at?

Lisa Dust. All dust. Stars and planets and comets and moons . . . and us looking up at them.

Eve (*turning away*) Well, that's depressing.

Lisa Not when you think about it. Like, all the things we are and all the things we have and everything we know is . . . random collision. Dust turning back to dust. And here we are thinking and feeling and . . . loving each other. When you think about that . . . it's magic. Pure magic.

Lisa continues to look out through the telescope. Lights dim. Eve moves downstage looking out. The band plays 'Magical Times'. Elsewhere Danny digs with a trowel, plants a bed of yellow flowers: they glow like stars in the dark.

Eve I want to buy a bunch of flowers. Let's say I'm a person who likes to buy flowers – every week a couple of quid: two quid plus two quid plus two quid . . . But housing benefit's down and rent's up, wages are down and tax credits are down so I'm a person who can't afford flowers. So minus the flowers, no more flowers, not for me, or for next door or over the road. So minus the people who drive the flowers, who grow and cut and sell the flowers – minus some of them. Minus the things those people buy, minus their chocolate, or meat, or furniture, cut their expenditure, batten the hatches as minus breeds minus and cut breeds cut and the maths won't fit it to tidy 'in–out' columns – the maths is floating up in to the sky: minusing, looping, grinding, slowing . . . And nothing grows. Nothing grows.

Lights shift as Eve exits. Danny continues digging.

SCENE TWENTY
DIGGING

Danny kneels, planting flowers. Lisa approaches him, placard in hand reading REFUGEES WELCOME. *Danny looks at her, then back to his work.*

Lisa Are you not coming then?

Danny Am I what?

Lisa Only it's gonna be a big one. I thought maybe . . .

Danny I'm working, Lisa.

Lisa I know. Mum saw you doing the grass verges by the canal last week.

Danny I didn't see her.

Lisa They reckon on thousands today. It's been building up. You won't wanna miss it.

Danny You been going on your own?

Lisa I kept thinking you'd be there. At one of the meetings or . . .

Danny Maybe I'm sick of protests? Maybe I've got other things to worry about?

Lisa People are angry. Properly angry. Like you say: common grievances.

Danny Who cares what I say? Aren't I just some fella you used to live with?

Lisa You could join up later? If you've gotta work.

Danny I haven't seen you in over a month. Now you stroll up –

Lisa I've been looking for you. Went to the house – there were new people in the front room.

Danny Got myself a flat, didn't I?

Lisa No phone reception there? 'Cause I've been ringing.

Danny D'you not think it might hurt? Do you not think it might hurt *me*, all this? The first two days I sat watching the door.

Lisa I'm here now. We're here now.

Danny So what is it you want, Lisa? Alan can pay for your new life but I should be there to hold your hand when he's busy?

Lisa Alan's a dickhead. He voted for Cameron and he listens to Dire Straits.

Danny You made your bed – you know what they say.

She stares at him. Walks away. She stops suddenly, turning back.

Lisa Easier to be a loser, isn't it?

Danny Look, I'm sorry if you're pissed off but –

Lisa Always talking the big fight – truth be told it's more your thing to lay down and die.

Danny I don't need to hear this.

Lisa Yeah, go on, rise above. It's easier to be too good, too soft, too clever. Well you're not clever enough. You're not good *enough*.

Danny *I wasn't the one who walked out.*

Lisa You let her down, Danny. How can you not see that? You let *me* down.

Danny digs more angrily. Lisa watches him.

You know, I always thought I was missing things. 'Cause I never had holidays, or new stuff, never had a Dad and everyone knew that. Always felt like I was walking round with holes in me – like people could see through me. Except you start to realise, those things they said I was missing: they were the things *they* wanted. They were never the things I needed in the first place. And anyway I did have a dad. Didn't I?

Danny The things she said, and you just stood there . . .

Lisa I'm asking you a question, Danny.

Danny I can't talk to her.

Lisa Talk to *me*.

Danny It's too late.

Lisa You called me your kid.

Beat. He looks at her.

To her. You called me your little girl.

Danny Yeah.

Lisa *Am* I?

Danny Course you bloody are.

Lisa Then act like it. *Act like it.* Talk to *me*.

SCENE TWENTY-ONE
SETTLEMENT

The band plays 'Where's Your Soul?'. Low light. Alan sits in an armchair, a wine bottle beside him. Eve approaches, taking off her coat. She jumps when she sees him. He's slightly drunk.

Eve We were meant to go out, weren't we? I had to stay with my Mum.

Alan Three times this week.

Eve She launched herself at one of the nurses. Pulled out a chunk of her hair.

Alan You'd rather spend time in that mad house than here with me.

Eve No. No, I . . .

Alan That's okay. I could accept that. I could accept that you don't find me fascinating or charming. I could even accept that you don't fancy me much –

Eve (*turning to go*) I don't want to do this now.

Alan Don't you? Because I'm paying your bills. I'm paying the school bills and the hospital bills: aren't I at least due a little respect?

Eve Is that really what you want from me, Al? Respect?

Alan I saw you with him. This afternoon. The two of you sat in your crappy little café in town with your heads together. Gazing at each other over your instant coffee.

Eve Aren't I allowed to be in a room with him?

Alan The pair of you laughing behind my back . . .

Eve We only talked about Lisa. He has to see her –

Alan Do you not know how much I've done for you, Eve?

Eve I'm grateful.

Alan You're grateful when something needs paying for.

Eve *Yes.* (*Beat.*) What else did you think this'd be?

Alan I thought you needed caring for. I thought you'd let me care for you.

Eve I *can't.*

Alan (*moving close*) I love you, Eve.

Eve You don't even like me. You don't like the clothes I wear or the things I say or the way I say them –

Alan You can't know how much I love you.

Eve I'm money to you. That's what you like. I'm money in the bank as long as I've got nothing.

Alan You've got everything of mine.

Eve Nothing of my own. That's the way you want to keep it, isn't it?

Alan That's not fair.

Eve That's the way you want to keep me.

Alan I picked you up off the ground, Eve –

Eve Out of the kindness of your heart?

Alan Yes. Actually, *yes.*

Eve All the time counting what you'd get in return.

Alan Don't I deserve something in return?

Eve That's not kindness, that's a transaction.

Alan (*going to her*) Every good thing you have is from me. Every last thing you have of value –

Eve (*pushing him away*) Then I'm fucking impoverished.

Alan Christ Almighty . . . That's your failures talking, Eve. That's your weak-headed money-phobic –

Eve My failures?

Alan That's what landed you in the shit heap in the first place.

Eve Tell me about my failures, Alan.

Alan That's why you're here, isn't it? Because you fucked every other thing up?

Pause. She stares into him.

How about I write you a cheque to get out of my life?

Eve How 'bout you keep it?

Alan If you think I'm putting you all on the streets it's you who doesn't understand me.

Eve *Keep it.*

Alan You'd destitute yourself to spite me?

Eve It's nothing to do with you.

Alan You'll pull Lisa out of school? You'll pull your mother out of the home?

Eve *Keep it.*

Alan And you'll look your daughter in the eye after?

Eve *Yes.* Yes I will. (*Beat.*) Keep your money.

SCENE TWENTY-TWO
TOMORROW

Lights shift. The band plays 'Magical Times'. Eve, Lisa and Iris enter carrying bags, cases, a telescope. In the food bank Steph, Theresa and Faisa are sorting food into boxes.

Lisa (*sung*)
These are magical times, rootless and wild
We are dancing unbound, unruled by the tides
I see ghosts of stars in a rolling sky
These are magical times, and where am I?

Music continues as Iris and Lisa sit on their cases. Eve approaches the food bank as Steph comes out with a cigarette. Seeing Eve, Steph turns back inside. Eve sits on the floor, waits.

Eve/Iris/Lisa (*sung*)
These are wondrous days when planets align
Sun and moon kiss and the dark swallows fire
I see silver and gold scattered high and wide
These are magical times, and where am I?

There are men singing songs from space
And I'm gravity, I'm endless weight
I saw the sky alight, too late
A million years ago
A million miles away

These are magical times, and where am I?

Music continues, swells, fades. Steph returns carrying a pile of boxes.

Steph We need this doorway clear for Health and Safety.

Eve You alright, Steph?

Steph No I'm not, I'm busy. Too busy for whatever display this is.

Eve I've got a voucher.

Steph Maybe I should help you then. Or maybe I should just fuck off like you told me.

Eve Remember in primary, like if I swore at you or you broke something of mine, or we wound each other up, we'd work out what we owed.

Steph There's people inside who need me, Eve – who aren't too proud to admit it.

Eve You remember, I'd give you ten penny sweets to make up for tripping you over. Or you'd let me ride your bike to make up for spilling my chips. All that nonsense . . .

Steph Nonsense, yeah.

Eve Well, I'll do anything for you now, Steph. Anything. I'll work all your shifts for no pay. I'll add up all the drinks and fags and crisps I've ever scrounged off you and pay you back in instalments. I'll let you have any of my clothes on an unlimited loan . . . I'll run round this car park with me knickers over my head –

Steph Do you not think I've had stuff to cope with? The shop closing, the bank account emptying, the kids freaking out. Did you not think while you were having your martyred episode that I was wading through all the same miserable shit?

Eve What can I do, Steph?

Steph I don't want you to *do* anything – I just want *you*. You silly mare. I want my mate.

Eve starts to cry. Steph goes to her, pulls her up off the floor.

Come here – the state of you . . . (*Wiping her face.*) Like a drowned panda.

Eve We haven't got anywhere to go, Steph.

Steph Course you fuckin' have.

She hugs Eve. Lights shift. Lisa and Iris are still sitting on their cases waiting for Eve. Lisa looks through her telescope at the city.

Iris What'll we do tomorrow?

Lisa Whatever you like. (*Pointing.*) We'll climb up the top of that cathedral. Jump off and fly round the city if you want. Swoop down over Chinatown, follow the river and out to sea.

Iris And what if it rains?

Lisa No bother. We'll go up over the clouds. Fly right to Ireland and back for teatime.

Iris *Will* we?

Lisa nods. Iris looks delighted at this. Her smile fades. Beat.

And what'll we do tomorrow?

SCENE TWENTY-THREE
POVERTY KNOCKS

Danny sits on a kerb with a placard: END AUSTERITY. *The band plays 'Whole Again'. The staff and Steph enter humming, holding placards:* SAVE LIVERPOOL WOMEN'S HOSPITAL, NO MORE NHS CUTS, *etc. Steph, Theresa and Faisa are arm in arm. Gabi and Paul hold hands. Rhythms build, speed up – whistles, drums, shakers added. Bryn catches sight of Ismael, approaches him, searches in his pocket, holds up the gold watch. Ismael looks at it in surprise.*

Ismael It's not mine.

Bryn (*nodding*) Cash Converters on Smithdown Road?

Ismael takes the watch, looks closer at it.

I've started on the taxis. Decent money if you never sleep.

Ismael (*handing he watch back*) It was never mine. I just wore it a while.

Bryn Take it.

Ismael (*walking away*) You think I can afford to keep that right now? That's two hundred pounds: take it and spend it.

Bryn (*pursuing*) No. I'll keep it for you. And when you can afford to keep it – you come to me. You come right to me.

Ismael nods, smiles at him. New chants rise up as they join the others: 'No ifs, no buts, no more cuts!' Eve, Iris and Lisa enter. Eve sees Danny, goes and sits beside him.

Danny Evie Brennan at a protest . . . It's been a while.

Eve It's not a secret club, Danny: anyone's allowed.

Danny (*glancing at her*) You look alright. Better than you did.

Eve Council got us in a hostel. 'Emergency housing'. The decor's a bleeding emergency: sixties curtains and eighties carpets – Mum thinks she's gone back in time.

Danny How's she doing?

Eve Worse. Then better. Then worse. (*Beat.*) She's asked after you a few times.

Danny She hasn't.

Eve She misses you.

Danny And you?

Beat.

Eve I *was* happy. I was happy for a long time.

Danny Don't say it like that – like it's over.

Eve You didn't choose me, Danny. Not just that once: whenever it mattered, you didn't choose me.

Danny I'll choose you for the rest of your life if you let me.

Eve (*getting up, walking away.*) Prove it.

Danny How do I do that?

Eve Work it out for yourself, Dan. Prove it.

He stands, follows Eve as she joins the others. Music builds: stamping, clapping, chanting: 'Out, out, Tories out!' Applause, whistles blow, as Steph pushes through, climbing on to a platform, facing out, speaking in a mic.

Steph Thanks every single one of you for coming. You pull together one of these things, you think it's gonna be one man and his dog. But you're all here and . . . Good fucking on you. 'Cause if they want to take our hospital they'll have to go through *us* – yeah?

The others cheer, stamp, whistle. Steph looks around, lost for words suddenly.

No more cuts! (*Stepping down.*) Sorry for swearing.

The others keep on chanting 'No more cuts', wanting more. Eve looks at Lisa, who's speaking in Iris's ear, calming her. She catches Lisa's eye, moves to the platform.

Eve (*joining the chant*) No more cuts! No more cuts! (*Shouting over the chants.*) I'm looking at a lot of angry faces. Maybe you're angry that you're here at all. Maybe you're angry you have to argue and protest for Accident and Emergency, and looking after old people and babies. (*Gesturing to the placards.*) A hospital like this one . . . *Babies.* (*She stares around her.*) You might be angry 'cause you're talking and talking and no one hears and the TV and the internet's clogged with noise, with politicians telling us we're lucky, telling us to grin and bear it, selling us their lies and their bad maths. They're selling us bad maths and I'm angry. I'm *so angry*. I'm angry at everything I can't help and can't fix and I haven't got the answers . . . But we know the right questions. Don't we? . . . When did we get forgotten? When did we get discarded? How did things get so painful and so stressful and so . . . disappointing? (*Beat.*) There's a whisper and a shout in this city, in this country. It tells us to be ashamed of our losses, to call these things our faults and call our unhappiness due punishment. Well it isn't. It *isn't*. And every day we accept those lies we betray ourselves. We give ourselves away, we . . . My mum used to say: 'Sell your knickers before you sell your pride. If they take your pride, they've taken you.' But they won't take us. They can't catch us. Because we're cleverer than them. And we're angrier than them. Because we don't believe their mantras. We are not Thatcher's children. There are holes in their maths and we can see through them. Our sums are not their sums.

The others roar in support. They move around Eve, people banging drums, blowing whistles. Lisa pulls Eve down and gives her a hug. A song emerges from the explosion of noise.

Theresa (*sung*)
When you're playing your games of poker and risk
When you're drawing the blinds and stacking your chips

Steph/Faisa/Gabi (*sung*)
When you're throwing your hand and cashing your cheque
While out in the streets they're paying your debt

All (*sung*)
I heard a rumour we're all winners now

If we'll scrap for our dinner and laugh while we drown
If we'll play sink or swim while the losers go down
All of us then will be sailors
All of us then will be sailors

Elsewhere Alan stands alone.

Alan (*sung*)
When the day breaks in with an ageing face
When breathing in is a breathless race

All (*sung*)
When nothing you own is your own when your place
Is somewhere below the line tucked away

Repeat chorus.

Eve/Lisa/Danny/Iris
Inside the walls and under the ground
In all of the graveyards in all of the towns
Sure as the stroke of a time-worn clock
Close as your heartbeat
Poverty knocks

The music quietens, voices continue as soft harmonies as lights close in on Eve.

Eve I'm a numbers person. I'm made of numbers. There are nine billion cells inside the human heart, dying faster than they can regenerate. Every time I draw breath five hundred million stars are born and die, and we are not a calculation. We're a flash of light across the sky. Too brief and too brilliant to measure. I am water and gas and flesh and bone; I am ten thousand trillion atoms dancing. And I am not the sum of my parts.

The band takes up the song loudly again with a blast of a lead instrument.

All (*sung*)
I heard a rumour we're all winners now
If we'll scrap for our dinner and laugh while we drown
If we'll play sink or swim while the losers go down
All of us then will be sailors
All of us then will be sailors

When you're playing your games of poker and risk
(Knock, knock, knocking)
When you're drawing the blinds and stacking your chips
(Knock, knock, knocking)
When you're throwing your hand and cashing your cheque
(Knock, knock, knocking)
While out in the streets they're paying your debt
Watch out the boat is a-rocking
Watch out the boat is a-rocking

Repeat.

Poverty knocks, knocks, knocks . . .

Eve takes Lisa and Iris's hands as they sing, as music intensifies, as others raise their fists in the air. Voices rise in layers. The band brings the music to a crescendo. Lights down.

End.